THE SIX SENSES
COOKBOOK

THE SIX SENSES
COOKBOOK

CHEFS OF THE SIX SENSES RESORTS & SPAS / Recipes
JÖRG SUNDERMANN / Photography
AUN KOH / Text

ARCHIPELAGO PRESS

Daybeds above the villas in Soneva Gili
provide a lofty, pleasant retreat.
OPPOSITE: A private sundeck at Soneva
Gili looks out over a vast expanse of
crystalline waters.

Managing Editor
MELISA TEO

Recipe Editor
KIM LEE

Assistant Editor
NG WEI CHIAN

Designer
CHAN HUI YEE

Production Manager
SIN KAM CHEONG

Photographer's Assistant
JONATHAN ANG

Project Director for Six Senses
RAYMOND HALL

Chefs
REMON ALPHENAAR
LIONEL VALLA
JAMES PATRICK TAWA
ASHLEY GODDARD
GREGORIO MONTANEZ
MICHAEL POUTAWA

Sommeliers
DAVE CALLOW
ALAIN RUFFIER
JULIAN PAGLIUCHI
ERIC ARTIERE

SIX SENSES RESORTS & SPAS
19/F Two Pacific Place, 142 Sukhumvit Road
Bangkok 10110, Thailand
www.sixsenses.com

First published in 2004 by
ARCHIPELAGO PRESS an imprint of
EDITIONS DIDIER MILLET PTE LTD
121 Telok Ayer Street
#03-01, Singapore 068590
www.edmbooks.com

Printed in Singapore.

© 2004 Editions Didier Millet Pte Ltd
Photography © Jörg Sundermann
Reprinted 2005

ISBN: 981-4155-31-4

CONTENTS

WHAT IS PARADISE?

The answer for Six Senses founder Sonu Shivdasani was the result of a simple urge to build a home in paradise for his wife. This marked the beginning of Six Senses, which includes the Soneva, Evason and Evason Hideaway brands.

It all began with Sonu wanting to take his wife Eva on holiday. More than that, he wanted to take her to paradise. So he took her to Goa, a place that had always captivated and enraptured him, hoping that the ex-Portuguese settlement would appeal similarly to his stunning Swedish bride. Unfortunately it didn't have quite the same effect, and Eva had to undertake the difficult task of trying to explain to her husband that her idea of paradise was somewhat different from his. In the end, she decided it would be easier to show him herself, and in the late 1980s, the two made their first of many journeys together to the Maldives.

For Sonu, the trip would be life-changing. The archipelago was all that Eva had promised it would be, and more. And by the time they returned to London, where the couple had a home in West Kensington, Sonu had decided that he wanted to build a home for himself and Eva in the Maldives.

At the time, however, the government of the Maldives was not allowing any foreigners to buy and develop property for their own private use. Property was only available for development to hotel companies, and each island was permitted to accommodate only one resort. Unlike most others who would have been fazed by the restrictions, Sonu was instead inspired and determined to bring his idea to fruition. And as luck would have it—for us, that is—Sonu had made some investments in a hotel company based in Thailand around this time.

Armed with their memorable holiday experience and a great deal of vision, Sonu and Eva decided to lease one of the abandoned islands in the Maldives, and began work on what would later become Soneva Fushi. Sonu set about building the business, while Eva personally designed the resort's interiors and furnishings. While working on Soneva Fushi, two things were of paramount importance to them. Firstly, they believed that there existed a breed of travellers who prized privacy, space and exclusivity above other qualities when choosing a place to stay. Their plan was to build fewer rooms on more space than neighbouring resorts, and to offer the very best service available. Guests would have butlers—amusingly called Mr or Miss Fridays—and their every need would be satisfied. The painstaking detail to attention can be seen in extra touches like cold, lemon-scented

Rustic terra-cotta urns dot the grounds of Soneva Gili, and the cool water within is used to soothe bare feet that have been out for too long in the sun.
OPPOSITE: Over-water villas at Soneva Gili are constructed with natural materials, and come with novel touches such as a private sundeck.

towels upon arrival and a choice of aromas (lemon grass or peppermint) for one's toiletries. These small, albeit highly persona,l touches all add up to become part of the larger Six Senses experience.

Secondly, they believed the resort could be built without damaging the environment. This belief in sustainable development has become a cornerstone of the Six Senses philosophy, and something that has set the group apart in the hospitality industry. While striving to create a luxurious experience for their guests, Sonu and Eva are equally committed to ensuring that their resorts don't damage the islands or other locations in which they are built. Building around an ancient tree or helping to protect endangered coral is all part of the process, if need be.

The Shivdasanis' two-fold approach, thus far, has been a complete success. Six Senses, which was formally established in 1995, has won numerous international awards for its various brands. While the essential philosophy of offering luxury of the highest standard with a natural, indigenous feel in design, architecture and service is constant across the company's properties, they are divided into three brands. The Soneva brand is the company's ultra-deluxe marque. Sonevas offer the very best in the most natural but comfortable surroundings. Evasons—which include the Ana Mandara brand as well—offer luxury vacation experiences in more contemporary design environments. Recently, this brand has been expanded with the launch of Evason Hideaways—an all-villa concept which emphasises romance and privacy. Part of each hotel but managed separately is the Six Senses Spa, committed to delivering unique and memorable spa services.

It is our pleasure to introduce to you within these pages not only each resort, but also recipes which have tantalised guests and turned many into return customers. Food and wine have an important role to play at Six Senses. After all, eating and drinking are two of the four most important activities undertaken by the average beach resort guest—the others being, of course, napping and sunning—and something on which gourmands Sonu and Eva place great importance.

Good food and good wine make happy guests. Whether it's a plate of chips by the poolside, a bowl of delicious Vietnamese phô, sumptuous Thai food eaten in an elegant restaurant overlooking the Andaman Sea, a private torch-lit dinner on a beach with sand beneath your feet and the freshest barbecued seafood on your plate, or a Maldivian curry spread, all of these and very much more are possible at the Six Senses properties. The food served can broadly be put into three categories. Most properties serve local specialities and basic international fare. All serve modern fusion dishes, which are key items at Six Senses. The blend of regional and international cuisines at Six Senses is, most people agree, a marriage made in heaven. The wine lists at each of the resorts are also well-developed and a source of pride for Sonu, himself a significant wine collector and connoisseur.

Most importantly, we feel that this book has come about thanks to people such as you. We've had so many requests for our recipes to be compiled into a book from guests who have enjoyed our food and felt that it was truly representative of Asia's best regional cuisines. With this volume of recipes, we've decided that they were right all along.

For guests, the book is long overdue and, we're sure, eagerly anticipated. For gourmands, we believe that you'll enjoy the innovative recipes the various chefs have chosen to share. And for Sonu and Eva, this book is a way of sharing their homes and vision of paradise with the rest of the world.

'No news, no shoes' encapsulates the Six Senses philosophy of getting closer to nature. On arrival, shoes are bagged and whisked away for the duration of your stay. OPPOSITE: The new Evason Hideaway at Ana Mandara is built in signature Six Senses style, seamlessly blending interiors with the natural exterior.

THE SCENE AT Malé International Airport after a plane lands is almost cinematic. The people emerging from the terminal could be archetypal movie characters: the bronzed adventure-seeking Australian surfers with their bleached hair, the Japanese ladies with their floppy straw hats, white socks and sneakers, along with the American playboy complete with Gucci sunglasses—even at night—and model in tow. It is not an uncommon sight to see hotel representatives waiting by the pier in front of the airport to match these visitors to the various resorts and hotels which have mushroomed of late across this island nation.

There is a wide choice of resort islands here. That means that every hotel and resort is situated on its own island. These resorts range from a basic beach shack to what must rank as some of the world's most exclusive and internationally acclaimed retreats.

Modern tourism in the Maldives began in 1972, when an Italian travel enthusiast, George Corbin, led the first organised tour group to the islands. Back then, barely 1,000 tourists set eyes on the surrounding crystal-clear waters. These days, however, thanks to visionary hoteliers like Sonu Shivdasani, the Maldives welcomes up to some 500,000 visitors a year.

It is an archipelago of 1,190 small islands spread over 98,000 square kilometres (approximately 37,839 square miles). With perfect weather, powdery white beaches, remarkable coral reefs, iridescent waters and spectacular marine life, the Maldives has all the natural ingredients which make up a picture-perfect tropical paradise.

It is also well-known as a great dive spot. Ninety-nine percent of the country is beneath the waters, which means underwater exploration is essential. Over three-quarters of the world's reef fish species can be found in the Maldives. These and a variety of other marine life populate the island's coral reefs, much of which were damaged by El Niño in May 1998, but are fortunately well on their way back to an amazingly speedy recovery.

In 1995, Soneva Fushi, the country's first super-luxe resort, opened its doors on the island of Kunfunadhoo, and a whole new group of well-heeled travellers started taking note of the Maldives. While past tourists to the archipelago tended to be budget travellers, surfers and divers, the islands soon became the destination of choice for the world's most discerning luxury travellers with the opening of Soneva Fushi.

Admittedly, Sonu and Eva Shivdasani took a big risk at the time in leasing the largest resort island in the archipelago, and then building only 42 villas on it. Later, they would build an additional 23, but even then, Soneva Fushi's total count of 65 villas is small compared to its neighbours. Most nearby resorts offered, both then and now, between 100 to 160 rooms, on smaller and what must have been much cheaper property. But the Shivdasanis were convinced that Soneva Fushi would work.

So far, their gamble has paid off. Travellers from all over the world have flown in to Malé International Airport before climbing aboard a

This cellar, housed below ground and often used for tastings and private dinners, is unique in the Maldives. OPPOSITE: Tasteful yet cosily furnished villas have been built without damage to the natural surroundings.

seaplane for the 111-kilometre (60-nautical mile) hop to Kunfunadhoo, in order for one to truly experience what the Shivdasanis have aptly called 'intelligent luxury'.

'Intelligent luxury' means a practical and realistic, yet creative approach to giving each guest the perfect holiday, without either damaging the environment or removing the illusion of the Robinson Crusoe experience. It means building a resort that is able to offer every amenity without appearing excessive.

It means contributing a percentage of revenue to environmental, social and educational programmes. It means that instead of televisions in your bathroom, each and every one of the 65 accommodations has its own private garden. It means that every villa has beach views. It means, most importantly, making every guest feel at peace with nature.

Arriving at Soneva Fushi is an experience unlike any other. From the seaplane, a small boat ferries you to the island. Along the way, hotel staff will ask you for your shoes. What might be an odd request anywhere else is perfectly in accordance with the Soneva Fushi philosophy of 'no news, no shoes'. Everyone walks around the grounds barefoot here.

It is just this kind of novel touch that has surprised and delighted guests since the hotel first opened, and Soneva Fushi has made a habit of catering to their every whim. A Pillow Menu offers a selection of 18 different pillows, and there is a cellar that represents over 400 wineries from all around the world.

Wine naturally should be well-accompanied. As expected, the food here is exceptional and the art of fusion cooking, incorporating a range of local flavours, seafood and fresh fruit and vegetables—almost all of which are grown on the island—has been perfected by the chefs of Soneva Fushi. When your stay draws to a close, the general manager is on hand to wave farewell, and you are ferried to the seaplane with a glass of Champagne, making a fitting end to a truly memorable experience.

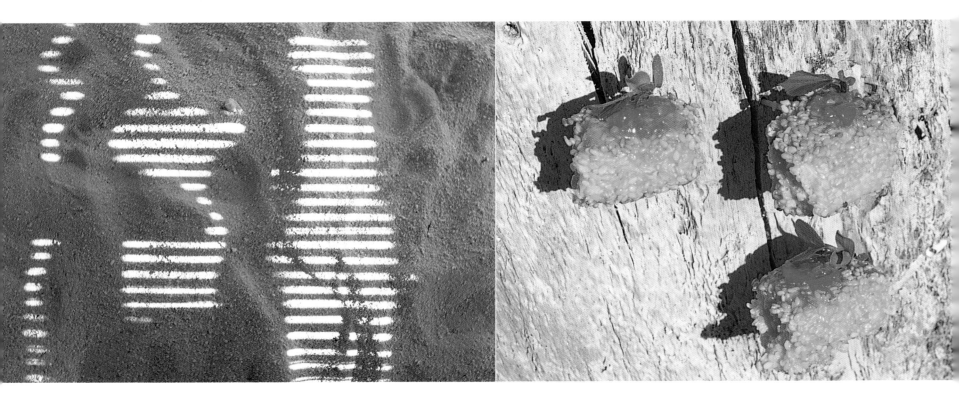

Powdery sands turn the island's 'no news, no shoes' philosophy into a pleasure; Pan-fried sesame-crusted ponzu salmon.
OPPOSITE (FROM LEFT): Deep-fried red lentil-crusted jumbo prawns; Pan-fried mustard-crusted scallops with capsicum salsa.

PAN-FRIED SESAME-CRUSTED PONZU SALMON Serves 8

PAN-FRIED SESAME-CRUSTED PONZU SALMON

160 ml / 5⅜ fl oz / ⅔ cup ponzu (citrus) vinegar
8 tsp soy sauce
650 g / 1 lb 7¼ oz Atlantic salmon fillet, cut into 16 cubes
80 g / 2¾ oz / 1½ cups white sesame seeds
8 egg yolks, beaten
Salt and pepper to taste
Olive oil for pan-frying

PAN-FRIED SESAME-CRUSTED PONZU SALMON Mix the ponzu vinegar and soy sauce in a bowl large enough to hold the fish. Marinate the salmon in the ponzu-soy mixture for 1 hour. Pour the sesame seeds on a plate. Dip the marinated salmon into the beaten egg yolk, then roll it in the sesame seeds. Pan-fry the sesame-coated salmon with olive oil until it just begins to brown. Remove from heat and allow to cool. Season to taste. TO SERVE Place the pan-fried salmon cubes on a platter with your choice of dipping sauces.

WINE 2001 Weingut Dr Heger Weissburgunder, Grand Cru, Baden, Germany

DEEP-FRIED RED LENTIL-CRUSTED PRAWNS Serves 8

DEEP-FRIED RED LENTIL-CRUSTED PRAWNS
60 g / 2⅛ oz onions, peeled and chopped
8 cloves garlic, peeled and chopped
Olive oil for frying
400 ml / 13½ fl oz / 1⅔ cups chicken stock
(see Basics)
160 g / 5⅝ oz / ¾ cup red lentils, soaked overnight
80 g / 2¾ oz / ⅓ cup tahini paste
Salt and pepper to taste
8 egg yolks, beaten
16 jumbo prawns, shells removed with tails intact
and deveined

DEEP-FRIED RED LENTIL-CRUSTED
PRAWNS Sauté the onions and garlic in a pot.
Add the stock and lentils and bring to a boil.
When the lentils are cooked, set aside to cool.
Add the tahini paste and season with salt and
pepper. Dip each prawn into the beaten egg
then roll in the lentils. Place the prawns gently
into hot oil and deep-fry until they float to the
surface. TO SERVE Place the deep-fried prawns
on a platter with your choice of dipping sauces.

WINE 2001 Weingut Dr Heger Weissburgunder,
Grand Cru, Baden, Germany

PAN-FRIED MUSTARD-CRUSTED SCALLOPS WITH CAPSICUM SALSA Serves 8

PAN-FRIED MUSTARD-CRUSTED SCALLOPS
160 g / 5⅝ oz / 3 cups mustard seeds
Olive oil for frying
5½ tbsp sweet mustard
16 scallops, cleaned
CAPSICUM SALSA
320 g / 11¼ oz whole red capsicums
40 g / 1⅜ oz red onions
5½ tbsp olive oil
8 tsp vinegar
Salt and pepper to taste

PAN-FRIED MUSTARD-CRUSTED SCALLOPS
In a pan, sauté the mustard seeds in a little oil and
allow to cool. Mix the cooled seeds with sweet
mustard in a bowl. Spread the mustard mixture
over the scallops. Pan-fry the coated scallops until
brown. CAPSICUM SALSA Preheat oven to
180°C / 350°F. Brush the capsicums and onions
with olive oil and roast on a baking tray until soft.
Remove skin and seeds, and chop the flesh into
small pieces. Mix with the vinegar and season with
salt and pepper. TO SERVE Top the scallops
with some salsa and present on a platter.

WINE 2001 Weingut Dr Heger Weissburgunder,
Grand Cru, Baden, Germany

ORANGE-INFUSED RAINBOW RUNNER & CELERIAC-POTATO MASH WITH SWEET CAPSICUM Serves 2

ORANGE-INFUSED RAINBOW RUNNER
2 (each about 180 g / 6⅜ oz) rainbow runner fillets
Salt and pepper to taste
Olive oil for frying
40 g / 1⅜ oz orange, peeled and sliced in rings
2 tsp chopped mint leaves
2 tsp orange juice

CELERIAC-POTATO MASH
400 ml / 13½ fl oz / 1⅔ cups chicken stock (see Basics)
160 g / 5⅝ oz celeriac, peeled and diced
160 g / 5⅝ oz potatoes, peeled and diced
60 ml / 2 fl oz / ¼ cup whipping cream
2 tsp butter
Salt and pepper to taste

SWEET CAPSICUM
2 whole red capsicums
4 tsp olive oil
2 cloves garlic, peeled and chopped
2 tsp fresh rosemary leaves
Salt and pepper to taste
200 ml / 6¾ fl oz / ⅞ cup chicken stock (see Basics)

SAUTEED MORNING GLORY
1 tsp chopped garlic
40 g / 1⅜ oz onion, peeled and chopped
4 tsp olive oil for frying
100 g / 3½ oz morning glory leaves
A few sprigs of fresh herbs for garnishing

ORANGE-INFUSED RAINBOW RUNNER
Preheat oven to 180°C / 350°F. Season the fish with salt and pepper. In a very hot pan, sear both sides with olive oil, then bake with the orange slices and mint leaves on a baking tray for 9 minutes until almost cooked. Remove the orange, squeezing the juice over the fish and set aside. CELERIAC-POTATO MASH Combine the stock, celeriac, and potatoes in a pot. Simmer until soft. Remove and drain. Process the solids in a blender until smooth. Return it to the pot and mix in the cream and butter. Season with salt and pepper. Keep warm. SWEET CAPSICUM Preheat oven to 140°C / 280°F. Brush the capsicums with oil and season with garlic, rosemary, salt and pepper. Bake on a greased baking tray until soft. When cool, peel and remove seeds. Place the flesh in a pot and simmer with stock until the liquid has reduced by half. Check seasoning. If it tastes bitter, add a little sugar. SAUTEED MORNING GLORY Sauté the garlic and onion in olive oil until fragrant. Add the morning glory and cook until wilted. TO SERVE Divide the capsicum between 2 plates. Top with morning glory, then top with the fish followed by the mash. Garnish with the fresh herbs.

WINE 2003 Haute-Cabrière Chardonnay Pinot Noir, Franschhoek, South Africa

SEARED OCEAN TUNA STEAK & CURRIED POTATO WITH GARLIC, GINGER & SOY SAUCE Serves 2

SEARED OCEAN TUNA STEAK
2 (each about 180 g / 6⅜ oz) tuna steaks
Salt and pepper to taste
8 tsp lime juice
Oil for frying

CURRIED POTATO
200 g / 7 oz potatoes, peeled and cut into 1-cm / 0.5-inch cubes
½ tsp chopped ginger
1 clove garlic, peeled and chopped
10 g / ⅜ oz onions, peeled and chopped
4 tsp olive oil
1½ tsp Madras curry powder
40 ml / 1⅜ fl oz / ⅛ cup coconut milk
2 curry leaves
Salt to taste

GINGER, GARLIC & SOY SAUCE
½ tsp chopped ginger
1 clove garlic, peeled and chopped
3 tsp olive oil
60 ml / 2 fl oz / ¼ cup dry white wine (chardonnay)
4 tsp soy sauce
Juice from 1 lime
Salt and pepper to taste

SAUTEED VEGETABLES
20 g / ¾ oz carrots, cut into thin strips
20 g / ¾ oz yellow zucchini, cut into thin strips
20 g / ¾ oz green zucchini, cut into thin strips
Olive oil for frying
40 g / 1⅜ oz morning glory leaves
A few sprigs of fresh herbs for garnishing

SEARED OCEAN TUNA STEAK Season the tuna steaks with salt, pepper and lime juice. In a very hot pan, sear the tuna on each side for 2 to 3 minutes for medium rare, or to desired doneness. CURRIED POTATO Cook the potatoes in a pot of boiling salted water. Sauté the ginger, garlic and onions in olive oil until the onions begin to caramelise. Add the potatoes and curry powder and continue to cook until the powder is evenly mixed and no longer smells raw. Add the coconut milk and curry leaves, and bring to a boil, then simmer for 5 minutes. Adjust with salt to taste. GINGER, GARLIC & SOY SAUCE In a pot, sauté the ginger and garlic in olive oil for 1 minute. Add the wine and simmer until the liquid is reduced by half. Season with soy sauce, lime juice, salt and pepper. SAUTEED VEGETABLES In a pan, sauté the carrot and zucchini strips in olive oil until cooked. Blanch the morning glory leaves in boiling salted water. TO SERVE Divide the potatoes between 2 plates. Arrange the vegetables around, then top with the tuna. Spoon the sauce around and garnish with fresh herbs.

WINE 1999 Santo Isidro de Pegões, Fontanário de Pegões Tinta, Portugal

Orange-infused rainbow runner and celeriac-potato mash with sweet capsicum.
OPPOSITE: Seared ocean tuna steak and curried potato with garlic, ginger and soy sauce.

BASIL-CRUSTED VEAL TENDERLOIN & YELLOW LENTIL RAGOUT WITH CINNAMON JUS Serves 2

YELLOW LENTIL RAGOUT
280 g / 9¾ oz / 1⅓ cups yellow lentils
1 clove garlic, peeled and chopped
40 g / 1⅜ oz red onions, peeled and chopped
40 g / 1⅜ oz tomatoes, peeled, seeds and pulp removed, and chopped
6 tsp olive oil
4 tsp chicken stock (see Basics)
8 tsp whipping cream
10 g / ⅜ oz basil leaves, cut into thin strips
Salt and pepper to taste

BASIL-CRUSTED VEAL TENDERLOIN
2 pcs (each about 230 g / 8⅛ oz) veal tenderloin
Salt and pepper to taste
8 tsp olive oil
8 tsp Dijon mustard
60 g / 2⅛ oz basil leaves, chopped

BABY CORN CONFIT
100 g / 3½ oz fresh baby corn
100 g / 3½ oz butter
200 ml / 6¾ fl oz / ⅞ cup chicken stock (see Basics)
6 tsp sugar
Salt and pepper to taste

CINNAMON JUS
120 ml / 4 fl oz / ½ cup port wine
1 cinnamon stick
160 ml / 5⅜ fl oz / ⅔ cup veal stock
Salt and pepper to taste

YELLOW LENTIL RAGOUT Soak the yellow lentils in cold water for 12 hours. Strain and let dry. In a pan, sauté them with the chopped garlic, onions and tomatoes in olive oil. Add the stock and simmer until nearly dry, then add the cream and basil. Stir this well and allow it to stand at room temperature. BASIL-CRUSTED VEAL TENDERLOIN Preheat oven to 180°C / 350°F. Season the veal tenderloin with salt and pepper. In a very hot pan, sear the veal in olive oil on all sides. Remove and smother with mustard, then coat with chopped basil and bake in the oven for about 12 minutes for medium-rare or to desired doneness. BABY CORN CONFIT Mix the corn, butter, stock and sugar in a pan and simmer until the corn is cooked. CINNAMON JUS In a small pot, combine the port wine and cinnamon stick and simmer until the liquid has reduced by half. Add the veal stock and simmer the mixture until it resembles a jus. Remove cinnamon stick and season with salt and pepper. TO SERVE Set each tenderloin on a bed of yellow lentil ragoût, place some baby corn confit on the side and drizzle the cinnamon jus around.

WINE 1999 Weingut Prieler Blaufränkisch, Austria

CHOCOLATE & MASCARPONE FRITTERS WITH ORANGE & GINGER COMPOTE Serves 2

CHOCOLATE & MASCARPONE FRITTERS
100 g / 3½ oz dark chocolate
100 g / 3½ oz mascarpone cheese
120 g / 4¼ oz / 1 cup plain flour
60 g / 2⅛ oz / ⅜ cup cornstarch
1 tsp bicarbonate of soda
240 ml / 8⅛ fl oz / 1 cup milk
4 tsp cocoa powder
80 g / 2⅞ oz / ⅜ cup sugar
Oil for deep-frying

ORANGE & GINGER COMPOTE
8 tsp orange juice
2 tsp soft light brown sugar
½ tsp cornstarch
2 oranges, peeled and sliced
3 tsp Cointreau
¼ tsp finely chopped ginger
A few strips of orange zest for garnishing

CHOCOLATE & MASCARPONE FRITTERS Melt the chocolate in a bain marie and whisk in the mascarpone cheese until smooth. Place dessert spoon-sized scoops of the mixture on a tray lined with greaseproof paper. Freeze for 2 hours. Combine the plain flour, cornstarch and bicarbonate of soda in a mixing bowl, add the milk and whisk until well mixed. Add the cocoa powder and whisk well. Let the mixture rest for 2 hours, then add the sugar and whisk until well mixed. Dip the frozen scoops of chocolate and mascarpone in the batter, then deep-fry in oil until the batter is crisp. ORANGE & GINGER COMPOTE Combine the orange juice, sugar and cornstarch in a pan and simmer until the mixture thickens. Add the oranges, Cointreau and ginger. Mix well. TO SERVE Garnish the fritters with orange zest and spoon the compôte around.

WINE 2000 Essensia Orange Muscat, Andrew Quady, Madera, California, USA

Sandy terraces with inviting daybeds make the perfect spots for spending an evening out in the open.
OPPOSITE (FROM LEFT): Chocolate and mascarpone fritters with orange and ginger compôte; Basil-crusted veal tenderloin and yellow lentil ragoût with cinnamon jus.

Tomato soup with chickpea and potato dumplings.
OPPOSITE (FROM REAR): Hot melting chocolate pudding with mirin and ginger sabayon; Herb-crusted Maldivian white tuna, orange-infused chèvre and curried papaya chutney.

TOMATO SOUP WITH CHICKPEA & POTATO DUMPLINGS Serves 2

TOMATO SOUP
400 g / 14⅛ oz tomatoes, peeled, seeds and pulp removed, and chopped
120 g / 4¼ oz white onions, peeled and coarsely chopped
2 cloves garlic, peeled and coarsely chopped
10 g / ⅜ oz basil leaves
10 g / ⅜ oz oregano leaves
10 g / ⅜ oz rosemary leaves
Salt and pepper to taste
CHICKPEA & POTATO DUMPLINGS
10 g / ⅜ oz chickpeas, soaked overnight
10 g / ⅜ oz potatoes, peeled and diced
40 ml / 1⅜ fl oz / ⅛ cup vegetable stock (see Basics)
2 sheets rice paper
Salt and pepper to taste
2 strips nori
1 tomato, cut into 4 thin wedges for garnishing

TOMATO SOUP Process the tomatoes, onions, garlic, basil, oregano and rosemary in a blender until smooth. Sieve the mixture by letting it drain naturally through a muslin cloth or fine-mesh sieve for up to 12 hours in the refrigerator. Place the liquid in a pot and bring to a boil. Remove any froth that may accumulate on the surface of the soup. Season with salt and pepper. CHICKPEA & POTATO DUMPLINGS Boil the chickpeas and potatoes in vegetable stock until soft. Drain. When cool, process the solids in a blender to form a smooth paste. Season with salt and pepper. Soak the sheets of rice paper in cold water until they turn white, then place them on a dry cloth to absorb the excess water. Place half the potato and chickpea paste in the middle of a sheet of rice paper and gather the edges and sides neatly into a parcel. Bind the parcel with a strip of nori and seal by wetting where the nori overlaps. Prepare another parcel with the remaining ingredients. TO SERVE Place a rice parcel in each bowl of hot soup. Garnish with tomato wedges.

WINE 1997 Torrelongares Reserva, Carinena, Spain

HOT MELTING CHOCOLATE PUDDING WITH MIRIN & GINGER SABAYON Serves 2

HOT MELTING CHOCOLATE PUDDING
1 egg
6 tsp sugar
70 g / 2½ oz butter, melted
10 g / ⅜ oz dark chocolate, melted
4 tsp plain flour
1 tsp butter for preparing soufflé moulds
FILLING
50 ml / 1¾ fl oz / ¼ cup whipping cream
50 g / 1¾ oz dark chocolate, chopped
MIRIN & GINGER SABAYON
1 egg
1 egg yolk
2 tsp sugar
1 tsp mirin
¼ tsp chopped candied ginger
2 strips candied orange peel for garnishing

HOT MELTING CHOCOLATE PUDDING Whisk the egg and sugar until creamy. Add the butter and chocolate and whisk until well mixed. Fold in the flour. Pour the mixture into 2 buttered soufflé moulds and freeze for 1 hour. FILLING Heat the cream in a pan to just below boiling point. Add the chocolate and whisk until smooth. Preheat oven to 180°C / 350°F. Remove the pudding from the freezer. Scoop a spoonful out from the centre of each pudding and fill the hole with the filling mixture. Cover the filling with the scoop of pudding removed earlier. Bake for 10 to 12 minutes. MIRIN & GINGER SABAYON Place a bowl over a basin of hot water and whisk the egg and egg yolk in the bowl. Add the sugar and whisk, then add the mirin and whisk until it emulsifies and becomes sabayon. Add chopped sweet ginger and mix well. TO SERVE Pour the sabayon on 2 plates. Remove the pudding from its mould and place it on the sabayon. Garnish with the candied orange peel.

WINE 2001 Elysium Black Muscat, Andrew Quady, Madera, California, USA

HERB-CRUSTED MALDIVIAN WHITE TUNA, ORANGE-INFUSED CHEVRE & CURRIED PAPAYA CHUTNEY

Serves 2

HERB-CRUSTED MALDIVIAN WHITE TUNA
20 g / ¾ oz coriander leaves, chopped
20 g / ¾ oz galangal, chopped
20 g / ¾ oz lemon grass, chopped
20 g / ¾ oz kaffir lime leaves, chopped
Salt and pepper to taste
200 g / 7 oz white tuna fillet
Olive oil for frying

ORANGE-INFUSED CHEVRE
4 oranges
6 tsp white port wine
20 g / ¾ oz shallots, chopped
100 g / 3½ oz chèvre (French goat cheese)

CURRIED PAPAYA CHUTNEY
1 tsp curry powder
5 g / ⅛ oz ginger, peeled and chopped
1 clove garlic, peeled and chopped
8 tsp olive oil
100 g / 3½ oz papaya, cut into thin strips
80 g / 2⅞ oz / ⅓ cup sugar
5½ tbsp white rice vinegar
A few sprigs of fresh herbs for garnishing

HERB-CRUSTED MALDIVIAN WHITE TUNA Mix the chopped herbs with salt and pepper and roll the tuna in the mixture. In a very hot pan, sear the tuna in olive oil for 2 to 3 minutes on each side, keeping the centre rare. When cool, slice it into 4 portions. **ORANGE-INFUSED CHÈVRE** Preheat oven to 120°C / 250°F. Peel the oranges and dry the zest in the oven overnight. Extract the juice from the oranges and discard the pulp. Combine the juice, port wine and shallots in a small pot and simmer until the mixture achieves the consistency of a thick syrup. When cool, mix it well with the chèvre. Process the dried orange zest in a blender until powdery. Sprinkle the powder over the chèvre mixture and cover well. **CURRIED PAPAYA CHUTNEY** Sauté the curry powder, ginger and garlic in olive oil until golden brown. Add the papaya strips and mix well, then add the sugar and white vinegar. Simmer until the mixture caramelises. **TO SERVE** Divide the papaya chutney between 2 plates. Top each serving with a layer of chèvre followed by a portion of herb-crusted tuna. Top with another layer of chèvre followed by the final portions of tuna. Garnish with the fresh herbs.

WINE 2002 Saint Clair Sauvignon Blanc, Malborough, New Zealand

COCONUT CAPPUCCINO & ROAST CHICKEN WITH TRUFFLES Serves 2

COCONUT CAPPUCCINO
300 ml / 10⅛ fl oz / 1¼ cups coconut milk
100 ml / 3⅜ fl oz / ⅜ cup chicken stock (see Basics)
1 tsp white truffle oil
½ tsp rosemary oil
Salt and pepper to taste
ROAST CHICKEN
60 g / 2⅛ oz chicken breast
2 thin slices of black truffle for garnishing
2 sprigs coriander leaves for garnishing

COCONUT CAPPUCCINO Combine the coconut milk with the chicken stock in a pot and bring to a boil. Add the 2 oils and season with salt and pepper. Remove from heat and process the mixture in a blender to a foamy emulsion with no oil visible. ROAST CHICKEN Preheat oven to 160°C / 320°F. Season the chicken breast with salt and pepper, then roast in the oven for about 20 minutes until medium-rare (the chicken will finish cooking in the soup). TO SERVE Slice the chicken and place in 2 soup plates. Pour the hot soup into the plates and garnish each with a slice of truffle and coriander sprigs.

WINE 2001 Misty Peak Pedro Jiminez, Limari Valley, Chile

CUMIN-COATED BEEF TENDERLOIN WITH MADRAS CURRY SAUCE Serves 2

CUMIN-COATED BEEF TENDERLOIN
2 pcs (each about 180 g / 6⅜ oz) beef tenderloin
Salt and pepper to taste
20 g / ¾ oz / ½ cup cumin seeds
Olive oil for frying
MADRAS CURRY SAUCE
1 clove garlic, peeled
Thumb-sized piece of ginger, peeled
1 tbsp finely diced onion
2 sprigs curry leaves
1 pandan leaf
1 tbsp cloves
1 tbsp cardamom seeds
1 cinnamon stick
1 tsp mustard seeds
1 tsp dill seed
Olive oil for frying
2 tsp Madras curry powder
½ tsp turmeric powder
60 ml / 2 fl oz / ¼ cup chicken stock (see Basics)
2½ tbsp coconut milk
Salt and pepper to taste
Juice from 1 lime
DEEP-FRIED POTATO STICKS
150 g / 5¼ oz potatoes, peeled and cut into sticks
Oil for deep-frying
Salt to taste

SAUTEED MORNING GLORY
10 shallots, peeled and diced
2 tsp olive oil
30 g / 1 oz morning glory leaves, washed and dried
Salt and pepper to taste
A few sprigs of fresh herbs for garnishing

CUMIN-COATED BEEF TENDERLOIN Preheat oven to 180°C / 350°F. Marinate the beef with salt and pepper, then roll them in cumin seeds. In a very hot pan, pan-fry the meat in the olive oil, sealing it on all sides. Remove and roll the beef in cumin seeds again. Place the meat on a greased roasting pan and roast in the oven for 12 minutes for a medium-rare steak or to desired doneness. MADRAS CURRY SAUCE Using a mortar and pestle, pound the garlic and ginger to make a paste. In a pot, lightly fry the paste, onion, curry and pandan leaves, and whole spices in a little olive oil until they begin to brown. Add the curry and turmeric powder and continue to sauté. Add the chicken stock and coconut milk, and cook for another 10 minutes or until the mixture begins to thicken. Do not let boil. Season with salt, pepper and lime juice. DEEP-FRIED POTATO STICKS Cook the potato sticks in boiling salted water until almost soft. Drain and cool. Just before serving, deep-fry the potato sticks until golden brown and crisp. Season with salt. SAUTEED MORNING GLORY In a wok, sauté the shallots in olive oil. Add the morning glory and sauté until the leaves wilt. Season with salt and pepper. TO SERVE Place each tenderloin steak in the middle of a plate. Pile potato sticks and morning glory leaves on top and drizzle Madras curry sauce around. Garnish with the fresh herbs.

WINE 2001 Château de St Cosme Gigondas, Louis Barriol, Rhône, France

ICED SOUFFLE OF YOGHURT & BERRIES WITH TOFFEE SAUCE Serves 2

ICED SOUFFLE OF YOGHURT & BERRIES
2 egg yolks
3 tsp sugar, dissolved in a little hot water
½ tsp gelatine, dissolved in a little hot water
5 tsp plain yoghurt
50 g / 1¾ oz / ½ cup wild berries
TOFFEE SAUCE
3 tsp water
35 g / 1¼ oz / ⅛ cup sugar
15 g / ½ oz butter
3 tsp brown sugar
3 tsp whipping cream
A few drops of vanilla essence
15 g / ½ oz deep-fried rice noodles for garnishing

ICED SOUFFLE OF YOGHURT & BERRIES In a mixing bowl, whisk the egg yolks, then add the sugar and gelatine and whisk again until light and fluffy. Fold in the yoghurt and berries and mix well. Pour into soufflé moulds and freeze for 3½ hours. TOFFEE SAUCE Combine the water and sugar in a pan and heat, stirring until the mixture turns caramel in colour. Remove from heat. Add butter and stir until the butter melts. Heat the mixture once more, then add the brown sugar and simmer until it dissolves completely. Remove from heat, add the cream and vanilla essence and mix well. TO SERVE Remove the iced soufflés from their moulds and onto plates. Spoon the toffee sauce over and around them. Garnish the iced soufflés with handfuls of deep-fried rice noodles.

WINE 2001 Inniskillin Gold Label Oak Aged Vidal Icewine, Okanagan, Canada

Crusoe chic bathrooms hide a multitude of modern amenities.
OPPOSITE (FROM LEFT): Coconut cappuccino and roast corn-fed chicken with truffles; Cumin-coated beef tenderloin with Madras curry sauce; Iced soufflé of yoghurt and berries with toffee sauce.

FATHU SATANI (LETTUCE, TOMATO & ONION SALAD)

Serves 4

100 g / 3⅓ oz organic lettuce leaves
1 tomato, diced
50 g / 1¾ oz red onions, peeled and thinly sliced
Juice from 1 lime
25 g / ⅞ oz fresh coconut, grated

Mix all the ingredients together. Season with salt and pepper. TO SERVE Present salad on a banana leaf.

GARUDHIYA (MALDIVIAN TUNA SOUP) Serves 4

300 g / 10½ oz tuna fish fillet, cubed
1 L / 1 pt 15 fl oz / 4¼ cups water
4 dried red chillies
4 black peppercorns
60 g / 2⅛ oz red onions, peeled and chopped
1 L / 1 pt 15 fl oz / 4¼ cups water
Few drops of lime juice
Salt and pepper to taste
1 lime, cut into wedges for garnishing

Combine all the ingredients, except the lime juice, salt and pepper, in a pot and boil for 20 minutes. Remove any froth that may accumulate on the soup's surface. Remove from heat and add the lime juice. Season with salt and pepper. TO SERVE Serve hot in a coconut shell garnished with a lime wedge.

FEHUNUMAS (MALDIVIAN-STYLE BAKED FISH) Serves 4

SPICE MIXTURE
40 g / 1⅜ oz dried red chilli
15 g / ½ oz red onion, peeled
1 tsp cumin seeds
2 curry leaves
½ tsp black peppercorns
Salt to taste
MALDIVIAN-STYLE BAKED FISH
4 (each about 150 g / 5¼ oz) tuna fillets
A few salad leaves for garnishing
1 tbsp pomegranate seeds for garnishing

SPICE MIXTURE Blend or pound all the spices into a smooth paste. MALDIVIAN-STYLE BAKED FISH Cut diagonal slits on the fish fillets and skewer them. Stuff the slits with the spice mixture and grill over hot coals or under a hot salamander on both sides until cooked. TO SERVE Remove skewers and place the fish in a coconut shell lined with salad leaves. Garnish with pomegranate seeds.

KATELA RIHA (SWEET POTATO CURRY) Serves 4

60 g / 2⅛ oz red onions, peeled and sliced
3 garlic cloves, peeled and sliced
4 curry leaves
1 (about 5 cm / 2 inches long) pandan leaf
Oil for frying
300 g / 10½ oz sweet potatoes, peeled and cubed
30 g / 1 oz semi-dried smoked tuna
1 L / 1 pt 15 fl oz / 4¼ cups coconut milk
500 ml / 1 pt 1 fl oz / 2⅛ cups water
3 tbsp curry powder
Salt and pepper to taste
60 ml / 2 fl oz / ¼ cup coconut cream

In a pan, fry the onions, garlic, curry and pandan leaves in a little oil until the onions caramelise. Add the sweet potatoes and fry lightly. Add the dried tuna, coconut milk, water, curry powder, salt and pepper. Boil over moderate heat until the sweet potatoes are well cooked and the sauce has thickened. Mash the sweet potato slightly and add the coconut cream. Check seasoning and remove from heat. TO SERVE Present the curry in a coconut shell.

Airy bedrooms allow guests to make the most of balmy sea breezes indoors. OPPOSITE (CLOCKWISE FROM LEFT): Fehunumas (Maldivian-style baked fish); Garudhiya (Maldivian tuna soup); Fathu satani (Lettuce, tomato and onion salad); Katela riha (Sweet potato curry); Mas roshi (Smoked tuna in pastry shell); Gabulhe (Dhal salad); Donkeyo kajoo (Banana fritters).

MAS ROSHI (SMOKED TUNA IN PASTRY SHELL) Serves 4

PASTRY
80 g / 2⅞ oz / ⅔ cup strong flour
40 g / 1⅜ oz margarine
2 tsp water
Salt and pepper to taste
FILLING
1 red onion, chopped
1 cherry pepper or red capsicum
2 curry leaves, chopped
Salt to taste
Juice of 1 lime
100 g / 3½ oz smoked tuna, flaked
50 g / 1¾ oz fresh coconut, grated

PASTRY Mix all the pastry ingredients. Knead well to get a smooth dough. FILLING Process the onion, cherry pepper, curry leaves, salt and lime juice in a blender to get a coarse mixture. Add tuna and coconut. Mix well. Shape pastry into small 'bowls'. Fill with the tuna mixture. Seal the pastry around it. Flatten the filled pastry to a circle or square about 8 cm / 3 inches across. Fry the pastry on both sides in a hot pan. TO SERVE Serve it hot in a coconut shell.

GABULHE (DHAL SALAD) Serves 4

100 g / 3½ oz red dhal or green gram, boiled
3 coconuts, grated
½ onion, peeled and sliced
1 green chilli
Few drops of lime juice
Salt and pepper to taste

Mix all the ingredients together. Season with salt and pepper. TO SERVE Serve in a coconut shell.

DONKEYO KAJOO (BANANA FRITTERS) Serves 4

6 medium bananas, peeled
4 tsp castor sugar
100 g / 3½ oz / ⅞ cup plain flour
¼ tsp of baking powder
A few drops of vanilla essence
Oil for deep-frying
50 g / 1¾ oz ginger, peeled and finely chopped
500 ml / 17 fl oz / 2⅛ cups water
300 g / 10½ oz / 1½ cups sugar
1 tsp cinnamon powder

Using a fork, mash the bananas with the sugar. Fold in the flour, baking powder and vanilla essence. Gently drop 1 tbsp of the paste into hot oil and fry until golden. Combine all the remaining ingredients in a pot and boil for 5 minutes. Strain. TO SERVE Serve fritters with syrup on the side.

Fresh herbs and vegetables grown on the island are an essential component of Soneva Fushi's dishes.
OPPOSITE (FROM TOP): Jasmine-flavoured bitter chocolate teacup with prune sorbet; Baked buckwheat crêpes with pumpkin-basil ragoût; Tandoor goat cheese and baked eggplant purée with mint coulis.

JASMINE-FLAVOURED BITTER CHOCOLATE TEACUP WITH PRUNE SORBET Serves 2

JASMINE-FLAVOURED BITTER CHOCOLATE TEACUP
120 ml / 4 fl oz / ½ cup double cream
10 g / ⅜ oz / ⅛ cup jasmine tea leaves
40 g / 1⅜ oz bitter dark chocolate, chopped
PRUNE SORBET
500 ml / 17 fl oz / 2⅛ cups prune juice or purée
5½ tbsp glucose syrup
2 sprigs mint leaves for garnishing

JASMINE-FLAVOURED BITTER CHOCOLATE TEACUP Heat the cream until just under boiling point. Remove from heat and add the tea leaves. Infuse for no more than 5 minutes. Strain the mixture into a bowl. Add the chocolate and stir until dissolved. Pour into teacups. Let them cool and refrigerate until set. PRUNE SORBET Boil the prune juice and add the glucose. Pour the mixture into an ice cream machine and follow the manufacturer's instructions. TO SERVE Place a scoop of prune sorbet on top of a chilled cup of bitter chocolate. Garnish each with a sprig of mint.

WINE 1998 Weingut Freiherr Heyl zu Herrnsheim Riesling Auslese (organic), Rheinhessen, Germany

BAKED BUCKWHEAT CREPES WITH PUMPKIN-BASIL RAGOUT Serves 2

BAKED BUCKWHEAT CREPES
200 g / 7 oz / 1¼ cup buckwheat flour
4 eggs
200 ml / 6¾ fl oz / ⅞ cup milk
2½ tbsp melted butter
2½ tbsp olive oil
Salt and pepper to taste
FILLING
200 g / 7 oz eggplant
4 cloves garlic
Olive oil for brushing and frying
20 g / ¾ oz onions, peeled and chopped
40 g / 1⅜ oz tomatoes, peeled, seeds and pulp removed, and chopped
40 g / 1⅜ oz spinach, chopped
Salt and pepper to taste
PUMPKIN-BASIL RAGOUT
300 g / 10½ oz pumpkin, skin removed and diced
80 g / 2⅞ oz onion, chopped
4 tsp sugar
2 tsp salt
200 ml / 6¾ fl oz / ⅞ cup chicken stock (see Basics)
6 tsp apple vinegar
2½ tbsp fresh cream
20 g / ¾ oz basil leaves, cut into strips
A few sprigs of basil for garnishing

BAKED BUCKWHEAT CREPES In a mixing bowl, mix the flour and eggs, then whisk in the milk. Let it rest for 1 hour in the fridge. Heat half the butter and olive oil in a pan. Pour a ladleful (about 30 to 40 ml / 1 to 1⅜ fl oz) of the batter onto the pan. Using the base of the ladle, spread the batter out thinly in a circular motion. When bubbles begin to break on the surface, flip the crêpe over to cook the other side. Remove from the pan and allow to cool. FILLING Preheat oven to 160°C / 320°F. Brush the eggplant and garlic cloves with oil and place in a greased baking pan. Roast until the eggplant softens. When cool, remove the skin and seeds from the eggplant and garlic, and dice coarsely. In a pan, sauté the onions and tomatoes in olive oil. When the onions caramelise, add the eggplant and cook until the mixture begins to thicken. Remove mixture from heat and add in the spinach. PUMPKIN-BASIL RAGOUT Combine all ingredients except the basil in a pot and simmer, stirring frequently, until the pumpkin softens. When the pumpkin is cooked, stir in the basil and allow the ragoût to cool. TO SERVE Fold the crêpes into quarters and stuff the pockets with the eggplant filling. Top with a dollop of ragoût. Garnish each with a sprig of basil.

WINE 2002 Domaine de la Bécassonne, André Brunel Côtes du Rhône Blanc, Rhône, France

TANDOOR GOAT CHEESE & BAKED EGGPLANT PUREE WITH MINT COULIS Serves 2

TANDOOR GOAT CHEESE
100 ml / 3½ oz / ½ cup yoghurt
½ tsp Kashmir red chilli powder
½ tsp ginger paste
½ tsp garlic paste
½ tsp lemon juice
A pinch of garam masala powder
½ tbsp Dijon mustard
A pinch of chat masala powder
150 g / 5¼ oz chèvre (French goat cheese), cut into 2 portions
Salt and pepper to taste
BAKED EGGPLANT PUREE
1 medium eggplant
2 cloves garlic, roasted, peeled and chopped
A few drops of lemon juice
Salt to taste
MINT COULIS
50 g / 1¾ oz mint leaves
1 medium red onion, peeled and chopped
100 ml / 3⅜ fl oz / ⅜ cup white wine vinegar
Sugar to taste
BEETROOT LEAVES
40 g / 1⅜ oz beetroot leaves
100 g / 3½ oz sun-dried tomatoes
2 tbsp plain yoghurt for garnishing
2 sprigs purple basil leaves for garnishing

TANDOOR GOAT CHEESE Mix all the ingredients except the goat cheese, salt and pepper in a pot and cook over low heat for 20 minutes. Season with salt and pepper. Remove from heat and allow to cool. Marinate the goat cheese with the tandoor mixture for 30 minutes. BAKED EGGPLANT PUREE Preheat oven to 200°C / 400°F and bake the whole eggplant until it softens. Remove and allow to cool. Peel the skin, remove the seeds and blend the flesh into a smooth paste. Season with the garlic, lemon juice and salt. MINT COULIS Boil the mint with the onion, vinegar and sugar, adding a little water if necessary. Cool and blend into a thick purée. BEETROOT LEAVES Blanch the beetroot leaves in boiling water just before serving. TO SERVE Arrange the goat cheese on 2 plates and top with eggplant purée and sun-dried tomatoes. Place the beetroot leaves around and garnish with a dollop of yoghurt and a sprig of purple basil each.

WINE 2001 Enate Barrique Fermented Chardonnay, Somontano, Spain

POACHED GINGER & LEMON GRASS JACKFISH WITH SOFT POLENTA & HONEY-CARROT SAUCE Serves 2

POACHED GINGER & LEMON GRASS JACKFISH
2 L / 3 pts 10 fl oz / 8½ cups fish or vegetable stock (see Basics)
20 g / ¾ oz ginger, peeled and sliced
2 stalks lemon grass, crushed
Salt and pepper to taste
2 (each about 180 g / 6⅜ oz) jackfish fillets, skinned
SOFT POLENTA
200 ml / 6¾ fl oz / ⅞ cup unsweetened soy milk
200 ml / 6¾ fl oz / ⅞ cup vegetable stock (see Basics)
200 g / 7 oz / 1 cup polenta
Salt and pepper to taste
HONEY-CARROT SAUCE
120 g / 4¼ oz carrots, peeled and diced
80 g / 2⅞ oz onions, peeled and diced
6 tsp olive oil
4 tsp chicken stock (see Basics)
4 tsp lavender honey
2 tsp whipping cream
Salt and pepper to taste
STEAMED ASPARAGUS
120 g / 4¼ oz Thai asparagus
Salt to taste
A few sprigs of fresh herbs for garnishing

POACHED GINGER & LEMON GRASS JACKFISH Combine the stock, ginger and lemon grass in a pot and bring to a boil. Season with salt and pepper. Add the jackfish and reduce the heat to a simmer. Simmer until fish is almost done (the fish will finish cooking in the residual heat). Remove, check seasoning and keep warm. SOFT POLENTA Combine the soy milk and stock in a pot and bring to a boil. Add the polenta and keep stirring on low heat until it thickens. Season to taste. HONEY-CARROT SAUCE In a small pot, sauté the carrots and onions in olive oil until golden. Add the stock and simmer until the carrots soften. Remove and process in a blender to get a purée. Return to the pot and add the honey and cream. Bring to a boil again and season with salt and pepper. STEAMED ASPARAGUS Season the asparagus with salt and steam until cooked. TO SERVE Spoon some polenta on each plate and top with asparagus. Place the fish on the asparagus. Spoon the honey-carrot sauce around and drizzle a little on the fish. Garnish with the fresh herbs.

WINE 1998 Weingut Bercher Scheurebe Kabinett Trocken (organic), Baden, Germany

Clear blue waters and coral surround the island of Kunfunadhoo.
OPPOSITE (CLOCKWISE FROM TOP LEFT): Poached ginger and lemon grass jackfish with soft polenta and honey-carrot sauce; Flourless chocolate cake with liquorice ice cream; Char-grilled organic vegetables.

CHAR-GRILLED ORGANIC VEGETABLES Serves 2

MARINADE
20 g / ¾ oz thyme leaves, chopped
100 ml / 3⅜ fl oz / ⅜ cup extra virgin olive oil
120 ml / 4 fl oz / ½ cup balsamic vinegar
Salt and pepper to taste
CHAR-GRILLED ORGANIC VEGETABLES
120 g / 4¼ oz mixed organic capsicums, seeds removed and sliced
60 g / 2⅛ oz organic eggplants, sliced
40 g / 1⅜ oz organic Thai asparagus
20 g / ¾ oz organic pumpkin, peeled and sliced
80 g / 2⅞ oz organic yellow zucchini, sliced
SALAD
30 g / 1 oz organic basil leaves
30 g / 1 oz organic mizuna leaves
20 g / ¾ oz organic rocket leaves
20 g / ¾ oz organic red coral lettuce leaves
Juice from 1 lemon
140 ml / 4½ fl oz / ½ cup extra virgin olive oil
Salt and pepper to taste

MARINADE Combine all the ingredients in a shallow dish and mix well. CHAR-GRILLED ORGANIC VEGETABLES Dip the vegetables in the marinade, then char-grill until cooked. Remove from heat and place them in an airtight container when cool. Pour the remaining marinade over the vegetables, seal the container and refrigerate. SALAD Place the salad leaves in a mixing bowl. Whisk the lemon juice with the olive oil and season with salt and pepper. TO SERVE Fill 2 plates with mixed salad leaves then top with the grilled vegetables. Drizzle with the dressing and toss well.

WINE 1995 Taurino Notarpanaro Vino da Tavola, Puglia, Italy

FLOURLESS CHOCOLATE CAKE WITH LIQUORICE ICE CREAM Serves 2

FLOURLESS CHOCOLATE CAKE
2 eggs
30 g / 1 oz / ⅛ cup sugar
200 g / 7 oz dark chocolate, melted
100 g / 3½ oz butter, melted
1 tsp butter for greasing soufflé moulds
LIQUORICE ICE CREAM
200 g / 7 oz / 1 cup sugar
12 egg yolks
1 L / 1 pt 15 fl oz / 4¼ cups milk
80 g / 2⅞ oz / ¾ cup liquorice
800 ml / 1 pt 8 fl oz / 3⅓ cups whipping cream
Chopped nuts for garnishing

FLOURLESS CHOCOLATE CAKE Preheat oven to 170°C / 340°F. Whisk the eggs and sugar until creamy. Mix in the melted chocolate and butter. Pour the mixture into buttered soufflé moulds and bake for about 25 to 30 minutes. Remove and allow to cool. LIQUORICE ICE CREAM Whisk the sugar and egg yolks until creamy. Bring the milk and liquorice to a boil, then add the egg and sugar mixture to the warm milk and continue to whisk without letting the mixture boil. Remove from the heat when the mixture begins to thicken. Add the cream slowly and mix well. Pour the mixture into an ice cream machine and follow the manufacturer's instructions. TO SERVE Place each piece of cake on a serving dish and top with a scoop of liquorice ice cream. Sprinkle with chopped nuts.

WINE 1997 Allesverloren Estate Port, Swartland, South Africa

THE SEVEN VILLAS that make up Crusoe Residences at Soneva Gili are appropriately named. Perched above the clear blue waters of the Indian Ocean, connected to neither pier nor land, these villas, accessible only by boat, offer unparalleled luxury and privacy. Imagine honeymooning in one of these impeccably designed, two-storey villas and sipping Champagne from an over-water sundeck with nothing but blue sea on all sides. The deck is also screened off from your closest neighbour who is some 40 metres (44 yards) away, so there's no need for modesty, no matter what time of day or night. The villa itself is a polished wooden fantasy on stilts. The living room, framed with a large picture window, is perfect for reading, eating, and just about anything one can think of doing on a tropical vacation.

The very large bathroom has two sinks—a necessity for all couples, no matter how long they've been together—a tub, a separate toilet, a gorgeous shower with a glass brick wall —accessible via a tiny bridge—and a ladder which leads down into the sea and extends to a privately enclosed 'water garden', in which couples have been known to linger. The villa has a deck upstairs as well, which is ideal for sunbathing, dining, and stargazing. If you are thirsty, the outdoor kitchenette is equipped with an espresso machine, and the wine cooler is stocked with a dozen of your favourite wines. Room service is a phone call away and will be delivered discreetly by boat. In essence, Crusoe Residences were built for couples who never want to leave their villas, and whose idea of the perfect holiday is sleeping, eating, drinking, soaking in the sun, swimming in the sea, and enjoying each other's company for days on end.

Of course, that might not be for everyone. Those wanting to venture onto land can stay at Soneva Gili's 37 other villas, which are all built over water but connected to the island of Lankanfushi by picturesque wooden walkways.

The resort's new 1,400-square metre (15,069-square foot) Private Reserve at Soneva Gili—probably the largest suite in the Indian Ocean—offers guests the finest in luxury and convenience with five separate buildings that house two master bedrooms plus accommodation for guests and two butlers, a private spa complete with steam room, sauna and two massage pavilions (indoor and outdoor), as well as an air-conditioned private gym and two boats.

Like its sister resort Soneva Fushi, Soneva Gili advocates a 'no news, no shoes' philosophy which, given the powder-soft sand that rings the small coral island, makes perfect sense. On really hot days, and for longer journeys—say from your villa to the spa—hop on one of the bicycles parked at your villa. Short rides are the order of the day, and you can bike the length of the island in less than 10 minutes.

Ride to the Six Senses spa for your jet lag recovery treatment. It is a blissful 20 minutes in the hands of highly competent therapists that will encourage you to book even more treatments at this world-class spa. When lying face down in the therapy room, a well-placed glass panel on the floor draws your gaze

With 29 Suites, eight two-bedroom Residences, seven Crusoe Residences and a sprawling Private Reserve, Soneva Gili has established itself as the prime spot at which to kick back and relax in the Maldives.

directly to the dazzling marine life that has made the waters surrounding the Maldives famous, as opposed to staring at the timber floors or your therapist's feet.

Most visitors will want to get a lot closer to the fish, and should make their way to the water sports and dive centre. The Maldives offers fantastic diving and snorkelling opportunities. Book a one-day dive or spend a couple hours snorkelling over nearby reefs. Or if you fare better above water, try the Dhoni Sunset Cruise, a luxury sea-faring trip for two. Relax on reclining deck chairs with Champagne and canapés while being ferried around the island. A glass-bottomed dhoni affords views above and below water which are equally stunning.

Those who prefer the feel of dry land beneath their feet can view the sunset from the resort's main bar which is perched over the water. Enjoy perfectly made caipiriñas while the water laps serenely all around. For guests who still have not seen enough of the marine life, there is even a 'sunken' bar in the middle where you can see the fish through glass tables.

It goes without saying that one of the essences of a Six Senses resort is its exceptional cuisine. Visiting gourmets can satisfy their gustatory cravings with a variety of incredible creations. Just like sister resort Soneva Fushi, Soneva Gili has its own vegetable garden, and the fresh salads and other delicious greens you will sample are all organically grown. Similarly, all the seafood served on the island is fresh from the sea. The fish is line-caught, using traditional fishing rod techniques.

After a cool cocktail in the bar, head to the main restaurant, where the chefs really shine. Combining the ingredients of the region with classic European elements, the kitchen team here has created a tasty South Asian-European menu that's been winning over guests since the resort's opening. Of course, as one would expect from a resort which emphasises quality service, any special request will be entertained as long as the produce is available.

BAKED NEW POTATO & SMOKED SALMON WITH DILL CREAM Serves 8

BAKED NEW POTATO
600 g / 1 lb 5⅛ oz / 1⅓ cups sea salt
750 g / 1 lb 10¼ oz new potatoes, washed
SMOKED SALMON
500 g / 1 lb 1⅝ oz smoked salmon, cut into strips
DILL CREAM
200 ml / 6¾ fl oz / ⅞ cup whipping cream
5 tsp lime juice
8 sprigs dill, chopped
2 stalks spring onions, chopped
1 tsp salt

BAKED NEW POTATO Preheat the oven to 180°C / 350°F. Pour the salt on an oven tray, place the potatoes on it and cover the tray with aluminium foil. Bake for about 30 minutes or until the potatoes can be easily pierced by a wooden skewer. When cool, cut one end off each potato to prepare a spot to stick in a skewer. SMOKED SALMON Fold each salmon strip and skewer it on a wooden skewer. DILL CREAM Whisk the cream, add lime juice, dill, spring onions and salt, and mix well. TO SERVE Dip the salmon into the dill cream and plant a skewer into each potato.

WINE 2002 Henschke Tilly's Vineyard Dry White, Barossa Valley, South Australia

PAN-FRIED MINI MALDIVIAN CRAB CAKES Serves 8

PAN-FRIED MINI MALDIVIAN CRAB CAKES
500 g / 1 lb 1⅝ oz / 3 cups crabmeat, shredded
12 sprigs coriander, chopped
120 g / 4¼ oz onions, peeled and chopped
140 g / 5 oz red and green capsicums, seeds removed and diced
80 g / 2⅞ oz / ½ cup plain flour
4 egg yolks
Salt and pepper to taste
½ tsp turmeric powder
100 ml / 3⅜ fl oz / ⅜ cup olive oil
A handful of dill for garnishing
120 ml /4 fl oz / ½ cup sweet chilli sauce

PAN-FRIED MINI MALDIVIAN CRAB CAKES Mix the crabmeat, coriander, onions and capsicums. Add the flour, yolks, salt, pepper and turmeric powder and mix into a paste. Shape the paste into small round patties about 3 cm / 1.2 inches wide and 1 cm / 0.5 inch thick. Pan-fry the patties in olive oil over gentle heat for 3 minutes on each side. TO SERVE Present the crab cakes on a bed of dill with chilli sauce on the side.

WINE 2000 Domaine de la Bécassonne, André Brunel Côtes du Rhône Blanc, Rhône, France

When Soneva Gili was opened in 2001, it was the first completely over-water villa resort in the Maldives.
OPPOSITE (CLOCKWISE FROM TOP LEFT): Baked new potato and smoked salmon with dill cream; Wahoo ceviche and fresh coriander on toast; Chicken katti roll; Pan-fried mini Maldivian crab cakes.

WAHOO CEVICHE & FRESH CORIANDER ON TOAST Serves 8

WAHOO CEVICHE
400 g / 14⅛ oz wahoo fillet (or any white, fat fish such as sea bass, sea bream or grouper)
4 tsp lime juice
40 ml / 1⅜ fl oz / ⅛ cup olive oil
120 g / 4¼ oz baby corn, halved and sliced thinly
80 g / 2⅞ oz white onions, peeled and sliced thinly
1½ tsp salt
1 tsp pepper
10 sprigs coriander, chopped
2 stalks spring onions, chopped
TOAST
16 thin slices French baguette, toasted
16 sprigs coriander leaves for garnishing

WAHOO CEVICHE Slice the wahoo into strips about 0.5 cm / 0.3 inch thick, 2 cm / 0.8 inch wide and 5 cm / 2 inches long. Combine the fish with all the remaining ingredients except the slices of French baguette and coriander leaves for garnishing and toss well. Set aside and allow the lime juice to 'cook' the fish for at least 3 minutes before serving. TO SERVE Divide the fish mixture into 16 equal portions. Drain excess moisture and place a portion on each slice of toast. Garnish each portion with a sprig of coriander leaves.

WINE 2001 Cervaro della Sala, IGT Umbria Antinori, Italy

CHICKEN KATTI ROLL Serves 8

FILLING
40 g / 1½ oz onions, peeled and sliced
10g / ⅜ oz garlic, peeled and chopped
10g / ⅜ oz ginger, peeled and chopped
50 ml / 1⅔ fl oz / ¼ cup corn oil
A pinch of turmeric powder
2 slices green chilli, finely chopped
300 g / 10½ oz chicken fillet, shredded
40 g / 1½ oz green capsicum, seeds removed and cut into thin strips
40 g / 1½ oz red capsicum, seeds removed and cut into thin strips
40 g / 1½ oz yellow capsicum, seeds removed and cut into thin strips
40 g / 1½ oz tomatoes, seeds and pulp removed, and julienned
A pinch of chat masala powder
Salt and pepper to taste
10g / ⅜ oz coriander, chopped
2 tsp lime juice
WRAP
4 chapattis (Indian flat bread)
4 sprigs coriander for garnishing

FILLING Sauté the onion, garlic and ginger in corn oil until the onion turns translucent. Add the turmeric powder and chillies and sauté for a further 3 minutes. Add the chicken, capsicums and tomatoes, and sauté until the chicken is cooked but still tender. Add the chat masala and season with salt and pepper. Add the chopped coriander and lime juice and toss well. WRAP Heat the chapattis on a hot griddle or in an oven. Divide the filling equally among the 4 chapattis and roll each chapatti around it tightly. TO SERVE Cut each roll diagonally and garnish with coriander sprigs.

WINE 1995 Château Clos des Jacobins, Saint-Émilion Grand Cru Classé Cordier, Bordeaux, France

Grilled yellow fin tuna steak and sautéed mixed vegetables with mango and pomegranate salsa.
OPPOSITE: Steamed roll of reef fish and mushrooms with coriander milk sauce.

GRILLED YELLOW FIN TUNA STEAK & SAUTEED MIXED VEGETABLES WITH MANGO & POMEGRANATE SALSA

Serves 2

MANGO & POMEGRANATE SALSA
50 g / 1¾ oz mango flesh, diced
30 g / 1 oz pomegranate seeds
1 green chilli, sliced
2 stalks spring onions, chopped
2 sprigs coriander, chopped
50 g / 1¾ oz cherry tomatoes, halved
200 ml / 3⅜ fl oz / ⅜ cup olive oil
SAUTEED MIXED VEGETABLES
80 g / 2⅞ oz green beans
80 g / 2⅞ oz baby carrots
60 g / 2⅛ oz green asparagus
100 g / 3½ oz snow peas
60 g / 2⅛ oz onions, peeled and chopped
Salt to taste
GRILLED YELLOW FIN TUNA STEAK
2 cloves garlic, peeled and sliced
4 sprigs oregano, chopped
2 tsp sea salt
Pepper to taste
4 tsp olive oil
2 (each about 200 g / 7 oz) yellow fin tuna steaks
A few sprigs of fresh herbs for garnishing

MANGO & POMEGRANATE SALSA Mix all the salsa ingredients together in a bowl. SAUTEED MIXED VEGETABLES Blanch the green beans, carrots, asparagus and snow peas in boiling salted water, then refresh them in iced water. Sauté the onions in olive oil until translucent, then add the vegetables and sauté until cooked. Season with salt. GRILLED YELLOW FIN TUNA STEAK Preheat the grill. Mix garlic, oregano, sea salt, pepper and olive oil in a bowl. Roll the fish in the mixture and grill for 2 minutes on each side. (If you don't have a grill, you may sear the fish in a hot pan.) TO SERVE Place the vegetables on 2 plates. Cut each tuna steak into 2 and place them on the vegetables. Pour the salsa over and garnish with fresh herbs.

WINE 2000 Verdicchio dei Castelli di Jesi Serra Fiorese, Cantine Garofoli, Marche, Italy

STEAMED ROLL OF REEF FISH & MUSHROOMS WITH CORIANDER MILK SAUCE

Serves 2

VEGETABLE TAGLIATELLE
140 g / 5 oz carrots
120 g / 4¼ oz green zucchini
Salt and pepper to taste
2 tbsp olive oil
STEAMED ROLL OF REEF FISH & MUSHROOMS
Juice from 100 g / 3½ oz lemons
300 g / 10½ oz button mushrooms, sliced
80 g / 2⅞ oz onions, peeled and sliced thinly
2 tsp olive oil
Salt and pepper to taste
400 g / 14⅛ oz white snapper or sole fillet
CORIANDER MILK SAUCE
160 ml / 5⅜ fl oz / ⅔ cup milk
A pinch of saffron
4 sprigs coriander, chopped
Salt to taste
FRIED LEEK
100 g / 3½ oz leeks, cut into thin strips
40 g / 1⅜ oz / ⅓ cup plain flour
Vegetable oil for deep-frying

VEGETABLE TAGLIATELLE Use a mandolin to slice the carrots and zucchini into thin strips. Season with salt, pepper and olive oil. STEAMED ROLL OF REEF FISH & MUSHROOMS Drizzle lemon juice over the mushrooms. Sauté the onions in olive oil until translucent, then add the mushrooms and cook over low heat until the mushrooms are done. Season with salt and pepper. Set aside to cool. In the meantime, slice the fish into strips about 15 cm / 6 inches long, 2.5 cm / 1 inch wide and 0.5 cm / 0.3 inch thick. Season with salt and pepper. Place 1 tsp of the mushrooms at one end of a strip and roll the fish around it. Secure the roll with a toothpick. Steam the rolls for about 5 minutes, then add the vegetable tagliatelle and steam for a further 2 minutes until the vegetables are cooked. CORIANDER MILK SAUCE Heat the milk to just under boiling point and add the saffron to give the milk a sunny colour. Remove from heat, then add the coriander and infuse for 5 minutes. Season with salt and strain. FRIED LEEK Roll the leek strips in flour and shake off excess. Deep-fry the strips in hot oil until they begin to brown. Transfer them to a sheet of kitchen paper to drain off excess oil and allow the strips to cook in the residual heat. TO SERVE Divide the vegetable tagliatelle into 2 portions and place each portion in the centre of a soup plate. Arrange the fish rolls on it, drizzle the sauce over and garnish with the fried leeks.

WINE 2002 Goldwater Dogpoint Sauvignon Blanc, Marlborough, New Zealand

Each villa comes with a screened-off over-water sundeck that offers its guests total privacy.
OPPOSITE (FROM TOP): Coconut and vanilla crème brûlée in coconut shell; Char-grilled chicken and artichoke basmati rice with balsamic vinegar jus.

CHAR-GRILLED CHICKEN & ARTICHOKE BASMATI RICE WITH BALSAMIC VINEGAR JUS Serves 2

CHAR-GRILLED CHICKEN
500 g / 1 lb 1⅝ oz corn-fed chicken thighs
4 tsp olive oil
Salt and pepper to taste
ARTICHOKE BASMATI RICE
120 g / 4¼ oz / ⅔ cups basmati rice
A pinch of saffron
4 artichoke hearts
1 red capsicum, seeds removed and diced
100 g / 3½ oz onions, peeled and chopped
100 ml / 3⅜ fl oz / ⅜ cup olive oil
6 sprigs dill, chopped
1 tsp salt
½ tsp pepper
BALSAMIC VINEGAR JUS
20 g / ¾ oz onions, peeled and chopped
4 tsp brown sugar
100 ml / 3⅜ fl oz / ⅜ cup olive oil
4 tsp balsamic vinegar
100 g / 3½ oz basil leaves, chopped
2 sprigs basil leaves for garnishing

CHAR-GRILLED CHICKEN Preheat the grill. Season the chicken with olive oil, salt and pepper, and grill (skin side down) for 10 minutes. ARTICHOKE BASMATI RICE Cook the rice and saffron in boiling salted water for exactly 10 minutes. Rinse with cold water and let it rest in a strainer. Boil the artichoke hearts in salted water for 15 minutes, drain and cut each heart into quarters. Sauté the capsicum and onions in olive oil until the onions turn translucent, then add the artichokes, rice, dill, salt and pepper and toss well. BALSAMIC VINEGAR JUS Gently heat the onions, sugar and olive oil in a pan. Stir until the onions caramelise. Add the vinegar and basil leaves and simmer until the mixture achieves the consistency of syrup. TO SERVE Place a portion of rice and artichokes on a plate and top with a chicken thigh. Drizzle the balsamic jus around and garnish with fresh basil leaves.

WINE 1999 Santenay Les Commes Roger Belland, Côtes de Beaune, Burgundy, France

COCONUT & VANILLA CREME BRULEE IN COCONUT SHELL Serves 4

COCONUT SHELLS
2 whole coconuts
COCONUT & VANILLA CREME BRULEE
150 g / 5½ oz / ¾ cup sugar
5 egg yolks
1 egg
500 ml / 17 fl oz / 2⅛ cups coconut milk
1 L / 1 pt 15 fl oz / 4¼ cups whipping cream
Seeds from 2 vanilla pods
200 g / 7 oz / 1 cup brown sugar

COCONUT SHELLS Cut the coconuts in half and scrape out the flesh. Reserve some of this flesh for garnishing. COCONUT & VANILLA CREME BRULEE Preheat the oven to 100°C / 212°F. Beat sugar, yolks and egg together until the mixture turns white and fluffy. Add the coconut milk, cream and vanilla seeds. Pour the mixture into the coconut halves and bake for 45 minutes. When cool, sprinkle a layer of brown sugar on top of each serving and caramelise the sugar with a hand-held gas torch. TO SERVE Serve in coconut halves with thin slices of coconut flesh on the side.

WINE 2001 Heggies Botrytis Riesling, Eden Valley, South Australia

ROASTED CRAYFISH TAIL & ZUCCHINI COMPOTE WITH FENNEL INFUSION & VANILLA OIL Serves 2

VANILLA OIL
Seeds from 1 vanilla pod
100 ml / 3⅜ fl oz / ⅜ cup olive oil
ZUCCHINI COMPOTE
300 g / 10½ oz zucchini, peeled
80 g / 2⅞ oz onions, peeled and chopped
4 tsp olive oil
6 sprigs dill, chopped
Salt and pepper to taste
ROASTED BLACK OLIVES
100 g / 3½ oz pitted kalamata olives, sliced thinly
100 ml / 3⅜ fl oz / ⅜ cup olive oil
FENNEL INFUSION
100 g / 3½ oz fennel, sliced
500 ml / 17½ fl oz / 2⅛ cups water
50 g / 1¾ oz onions, peeled and chopped
10 g / ⅜ oz garlic, peeled and coarsely chopped
1 tsp pastis
A pinch of turmeric powder
50 ml / 1¾ fl oz / ¼ cup olive oil
Salt to taste
ROASTED CRAYFISH TAIL
1.2 kg / 2 lb 10⅜ oz crayfish tails, halved lengthwise
Salt and pepper to taste
2 sprigs purple basil for garnishing

VANILLA OIL Infuse the olive oil with the vanilla seeds for at least a couple of days before using. ZUCCHINI COMPOTE Cut the zucchini into half lengthwise. Scoop out the seeds and dice the flesh. Sauté the onions in olive oil until translucent, then add the zucchini and cook over low heat until it softens. Remove from heat and mash with a fork. Mix the dill into the mash. Season with salt and pepper. ROASTED BLACK OLIVES Boil the olives in water for 5 minutes. Drain and sauté them in olive oil for 1 hour over low heat. FENNEL INFUSION In a saucepan, simmer the fennel, water, onions, garlic and pastis until the mixture reduces by half. Process the mixture with the turmeric powder in a blender until smooth. Strain and mix this with the olive oil. Season with salt. ROASTED CRAYFISH TAIL Preheat the grill. Season the crayfish with salt and pepper, then grill the shell side for 4 minutes. Turn the crayfish over and grill the cut side for 3 minutes. Season with salt and pepper. TO SERVE Divide the zucchini compôte and olives between 2 plates. Separate the meat of the crayfish from its shell about halfway down the tail and place the tails on the compôte. Pour the sauce around it and sprinkle some vanilla oil over. Garnish with purple basil.

WINE 2000 Michel Torino Altimus, Cafayate, Argentina

The island's fresh water infinity pool is the perfect place to laze around in, meet people and enjoy a cool cocktail. OPPOSITE (FROM LEFT): Roasted crayfish tail and zucchini compôte with fennel infusion and vanilla oil; Cappuccino of celery, leek and Spanish onion with pesto; Fruit sushi with raspberry and green tea coulis.

CAPPUCCINO OF CELERY, LEEK & SPANISH ONION WITH PESTO Serves 2

CAPPUCCINO OF CELERY, LEEK & SPANISH ONION
400 g / 14⅛ oz celery, peeled and chopped
100 g / 3½ oz leek, chopped
120 g / 4¼ oz white onions, peeled and chopped
50 ml / 3⅜ fl oz / ⅜ cup olive oil
1 L / 1 pt 15 fl oz / 4¼ cups chicken stock
(see Basics)
2 bay leaves
150 ml / 5 fl oz / ⅝ cup whipping cream
Salt and pepper to taste
PESTO
4 tsp pesto
6 tsp olive oil
100 ml / 3⅜ fl oz / ⅜ cup milk for steaming into froth
2 sprigs basil leaves for garnishing

CAPPUCCINO OF CELERY, LEEK & SPANISH ONION In a big pot, sauté the vegetables in olive oil until soft. Add chicken stock and bay leaves and slowly bring to a boil. Add the cream, mix well and simmer for 2 minutes. Season with salt and pepper. Process the mixture in a blender until smooth, then strain. PESTO Mix the pesto with olive oil. TO SERVE Pour the hot soup into 2 teacups. You may top the soup with milk whipped into froth by a coffee machine steamer or simply use a hand blender to process the remaining soup until frothy, then spoon the foam over the soup in the teacup. Drizzle with pesto and garnish with a basil leaf.

WINE 2001 Weingut Dr Heger Muskateller Spätlese, Ihringer Winklerberg, Baden, Germany

FRUIT SUSHI WITH RASPBERRY & GREEN TEA COULIS Serves 2

GINGER CONFIT
50 g / 1¾ oz Japanese pickled ginger
50 g / 1¾ oz / ¼ cup sugar
200 ml / 6¾ fl oz / ⅞ cup water
RASPBERRY & GREEN TEA COULIS
1 green tea bag
200 ml / 6¾ fl oz / ⅞ cup hot water
50 g / 1¾ oz / ¼ cup sugar
1 sprig mint leaves, finely sliced
50 g / 1¾ oz / ¼ cup raspberries
JELLY
2 gelatine leaves, soaked in cold water until soft
150 ml / 5 fl oz / ⅝ cup water
FRUIT SUSHI
300 g / 10½ oz / 1½ cups sushi rice
400 ml / 13½ fl oz / 1⅔ cups water
50 g / 1¾ oz / ¼ cup sugar
Seeds from 1 vanilla pod
30 g / 1 oz / 1 cup desiccated coconut
150 g / 5¼ oz kiwi fruit, peeled and sliced
60 g / 2⅛ oz strawberries, sliced
100 g / 3½ oz mango flesh, sliced
80 g / 2⅞ oz plums, seeds removed and sliced

GINGER CONFIT Boil the pickled ginger in salted water for 20 minutes. Drain and mix with the sugar. Let sit for 2 hours, then add the water and bring to a boil. Lower the heat and simmer for 5 minutes. RASPBERRY & GREEN TEA COULIS Infuse the hot water with the green tea bag for 5 minutes. Add the sugar and boil until it achieves the consistency of syrup. When cool, add mint leaves and raspberries, and process the mixture in a blender until smooth. JELLY Heat the water, dissolve the gelatine leaves in it. FRUIT SUSHI Cook the rice with 300 ml / 10⅛ fl oz / 1¼ cups of water in a rice cooker. Boil the remaining water with the sugar to make a syrup. Mix in the vanilla seeds. When the rice is cooked and still hot, mix in the syrup and desiccated coconut. Cover and let cool. When the rice is cool, wet your hands and take about 2 tbsp of it and shape into an oval block. Arrange slices of fruit on top and brush a coating of warm jelly over it. TO SERVE Arrange the fruit sushi on a plate and serve with the coulis and ginger confit on the side.

WINE 2000 Essensia Orange Muscat, Andrew Quady, Madera, California, USA

DEEP-FRIED SESAME-CRUSTED PRAWNS, GUACAMOLE & ORGANIC SALAD WITH BEETROOT VINAIGRETTE Serves 2

GUACAMOLE
400 g / 14⅛ oz avocado flesh, cut into chunks
240 ml / 8⅛ fl oz / 1 cup lime juice
Tabasco sauce to taste
2 cloves garlic, peeled
4 tsp olive oil
Salt to taste

BEETROOT VINAIGRETTE
120 g / 4¼ oz beetroot, cleaned but not peeled
2 tsp red wine vinegar
1 tsp salt
60 ml / 2 fl oz / ¼ cup olive oil
1 egg yolk

DEEP-FRIED SESAME-CRUSTED PRAWNS
1 egg yolk
Salt to taste
160 g / 5⅝ oz / 3 cups black sesame seeds
160 g / 5⅝ oz / 3 cups white sesame seeds
400 g / 14⅛ oz prawns, shelled (tails retained)
Vegetable oil for deep-frying

ORGANIC SALAD
3 organic mizuna leaves
2 organic lollo rosso leaves
4 organic rocket leaves
2 organic radicchio leaves

GUACAMOLE Process the avocado, lime juice, Tabasco sauce, garlic, olive oil and salt in a blender until smooth. BEETROOT VINAIGRETTE Preheat the oven to 180°C / 350°F. Wrap the beetroot in aluminium foil and bake for 40 minutes. When cool, peel and cut into wedges, then mash with the vinegar, salt and oil using a fork. Mix in the egg yolk. DEEP-FRIED SESAME-CRUSTED PRAWNS Beat the egg yolk with salt. In a separate bowl, mix the sesame seeds. Devein the prawns and coat them in egg wash followed by the sesame seeds. Deep-fry for 4 minutes. ORGANIC SALAD Combine the salad leaves in a bowl and toss well. TO SERVE Divide the salad, guacamole and prawns between 2 plates. Drizzle the vinaigrette on the salad and around the prawns.

WINE 2001 Yalumba The Virgilius Viognier, Eden Valley, South Australia

ROAST ANGUS BEEF TENDERLOIN & CELERY MOUSSELINE & CHIPS WITH PORT WINE & PORCINI JUS Serves 2

ROAST ANGUS BEEF TENDERLOIN
2 pcs (each about 250 g / 8⅞ oz) Angus beef tenderloin
2 tbsp vegetable oil
Sea salt and pepper to taste
PORT WINE & PORCINI JUS
100 g / 3½ oz dried porcini
4 tsp port wine
100 ml / 3⅜ fl oz / ⅜ cup veal stock (see Basics)
CELERY MOUSSELINE & CHIPS
600 g / 1 lb 5 oz celery
1 L / 1 pt 15 fl oz / 4¼ cups water
200 ml / 6¾ fl oz / ⅞ cup milk
Salt to taste
A pinch of nutmeg powder
100 g / 3½ oz butter
1 tsp white truffle oil
Vegetable oil for deep-frying
SAUTEED VEGETABLES
100 g / 3½ oz green beans
60 g / 2⅛ oz baby/young carrots
60 g / 2⅛ oz broccoli
2 cloves garlic, peeled and chopped
6 sprigs parsley, chopped
100 ml / 3⅜ fl oz / ⅜ cup olive oil
Sea salt and pepper to taste
2 sprigs parsley for garnishing
2 tbsp fried sliced garlic for garnishing
A few drops of olive oil for garnishing

ROAST ANGUS BEEF TENDERLOIN
Preheat the oven to 245°C / 475°F. Rub the beef with oil and pepper, then place it on a greased roasting pan. Roast in the oven for 15 minutes to seal its surfaces. Reduce the heat to 180°C / 350°F and roast for a further 15 minutes. This will give a rare roast, recommended for this dish. Sprinkle with salt. PORT WINE & PORCINI JUS Preheat the oven to 60°C / 140°F. Bake the dried porcini for 30 minutes. When cool, process in a blender until powdery. In a saucepan, simmer the port wine until it has reduced by half, then add the veal stock and porcini. Mix well and simmer until the mixture resembles a jus. Strain and reserve in pan. CELERY MOUSSELINE & CHIPS Peel 500 g / 1 lb 1⅝ oz of celery and boil in water and milk with salt until soft. You should be able to pierce a knife through it easily. Drain and process it in a blender with the nutmeg powder until smooth. Blend in the butter and truffle oil. Remove and keep warm in a bain marie until required. Cut the remaining celery into thin slices with a mandolin. Deep-fry in vegetable oil until crisp. SAUTEED VEGETABLES Blanch the vegetables in boiling salted water for 5 minutes. Refresh with iced water and sauté with garlic and parsley in olive oil for 2 minutes. Season with salt and pepper.

TO SERVE Divide the beef, vegetables and celery mousseline between 2 plates. Spoon the port wine and porcini jus over, then garnish with celery chips, parsley, fried garlic, a sprinkling of salt and pepper and a few drops of olive oil.

WINE 1999 Echeverria Family Reserve Cabernet Sauvignon, Molina, Chile

SPICED PINEAPPLE WITH KULFI ICE CREAM Serves 2

SPICED PINEAPPLE
500 g / 1 lb 1⅝ oz pineapple
1 L / 1 pt 15 fl oz / 4¼ cups water
250 g / 8⅞ oz / 1¼ cups sugar
Seeds from 2 vanilla pods (retain pods for garnishing)
1 star anise
1 small cinnamon stick
KULFI ICE CREAM
1 L / 1 pt 15 fl oz / 4¼ cups milk
A pinch of saffron
8 egg yolks
200 g / 7 oz / 1 cup sugar
400 ml / 13½ fl oz / 1⅔ cups condensed milk
200 g / 7 oz / 1½ cups pistachios, chopped
2 wafers for garnishing
2 sprigs mint for garnishing

SPICED PINEAPPLE Cut the pineapple in half lengthwise and trim away the skin, black spots and fibrous core. Boil the water and sugar to make a syrup. Add the vanilla seeds, star anise, cinnamon and pineapple. Simmer until the pineapple softens. KULFI ICE CREAM Bring the milk to a simmer and add the saffron. Remove from heat. In a bowl, beat the yolks with the sugar and add this to the hot milk. Return to heat and stir until it thickens. Add the condensed milk and pistachios, mix well and pour the mixture into an ice cream machine. Follow the manufacturer's directions. TO SERVE Cut the pineapple into thin slices and arrange them on 2 plates. Top with scoops of kulfi ice cream. Drizzle the pineapple syrup around. Garnish with wafers, mint leaves and vanilla pods.

WINE 1995 Schloss Halbturn Muskat Ottonel Beerenauslese, Burgenland, Austria

A hammock resting in the middle of a sandbank overlooks the hotel's own little island, marked by a single coconut tree. OPPOSITE (FROM TOP): Deep-fried sesame-crusted prawns, guacamole and organic salad with beetroot vinaigrette; Roast Angus beef tenderloin and celery mousseline and chips with port wine and porcini jus; Spiced pineapple with kulfi ice cream.

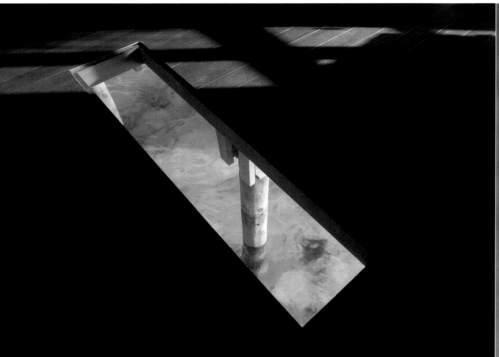

A glass panel on the floor of a Crusoe
Residence provides guests with the
visual treat of fish swimming underfoot;
Organic garden herb salad.
OPPOSITE (FROM LEFT): Seafood spaghetti
cooked in seawater; Hot chocolate
and Bailey's fondue.

ORGANIC GARDEN HERB SALAD Serves 4

ORGANIC GARDEN HERB SALAD
1 head organic lollo rosso
1 head organic radicchio
1 head organic frisée
1 head organic lettuce
10 organic mizuna leaves
20 organic rocket leaves
2 sprigs organic basil, crushed
2 sprigs organic mint, crushed
4 sprigs organic chives, chopped
80 g / 2⅞ oz organic carrots, diced
60 g / 2⅛ oz organic shallots, chopped
DRESSING
6 tsp lime juice
Salt and pepper to taste
100 ml / 3⅜ fl oz / ⅜ cup olive oil

ORGANIC GARDEN HERB SALAD Separate
the salad leaves from their heads and trim
their spines. Wash and dry the leaves then tear
them into bite-sized pieces. Combine them with
the basil, mint, chives, carrots and shallots in a
large serving bowl and toss well. DRESSING
Combine the lime juice, salt, pepper and olive oil
in a blender and process into a smooth emulsion.
TO SERVE Drizzle the dressing over the salad
and toss well.

WINE 2002 Groot Constantia Blanc de Noir
(Rose), Constantia, South Africa

SEAFOOD SPAGHETTI COOKED IN SEAWATER Serves 4

SEAFOOD SPAGHETTI
120 g / 4¼ oz onions, peeled and chopped
50 ml / 1¾ fl oz / ¼ cup olive oil
3 cloves garlic, peeled and sliced
400 g / 14⅛ oz crayfish tails, halved lengthwise
with shells intact
400 g / 14⅛ oz scampi
300 g / 10½ oz mussels
200 g / 7 oz calamari, cut into rings
5 tsp tomato paste
1 kg / 2 lb 3¼ oz tomatoes, peeled and chopped
200 ml / 6¾ fl oz / ⅞ cup white wine (chardonnay)
200 g / 7 oz dried spaghetti
2 L / 3 pts 10 fl oz / 8½ cups seawater
(if seawater is unavailable, substitute by boiling 2 L
/ 3 pts 10 fl oz / 8½ cups water with 4 tsp sea salt)
Salt and pepper to taste
4 sprigs basil
3 sprigs oregano, chopped
1 tsp chilli flakes

SEAFOOD SPAGHETTI In a big saucepan, sauté the onions in olive oil until translucent. Add the garlic, crayfish, scampi and mussels and cook for 5 minutes. Add the calamari, tomato paste and tomatoes and stir well. Add the white wine and simmer for 3 minutes. Next, add the spaghetti and simmer until it softens. Mix the spaghetti well with the other ingredients, then add 2 ladlefuls of seawater and bring the mixture to a boil. When it starts to dry, add more seawater and simmer until dry. Keep repeating this step until the spaghetti is cooked al dente. Check seasoning and adjust with salt and pepper to taste. If it is too salty, dilute with plain water and simmer until dry. TO SERVE Chop half the basil and sprinkle the chopped basil, oregano and chilli flakes over the spaghetti. Garnish with remaining basil sprigs.

WINE 2002 Enate Rosado Cabernet, Somontano, Spain

HOT CHOCOLATE & BAILEY'S FONDUE Serves 4

HOT CHOCOLATE & BAILEY'S FONDUE
300 g / 10½ oz dark chocolate
2 tsp Bailey's Irish Cream
ACCOMPANIMENTS
Juice from 2 lemons
1 large banana, sliced
10 pieces of palm leaves (such as banana leaves)
150 g / 5¼ oz kiwi fruit, peeled and sliced
250 g / 8⅞ oz strawberries, halved
250 g / 8⅞ oz mango flesh, cut into cubes
200 g / 7 oz plums, seeds removed and wedged
200 g / 7 oz Turkish delight
150 g / 5¼ oz marshmallows
80 g / 2⅞ oz coconut boondi
200 g / 7 oz cookies
200 g / 7 oz mud cake, cut into cubes

HOT CHOCOLATE & BAILEY'S FONDUE
Melt the chocolate in a bain marie, then mix in the Bailey's Irish Cream. ACCOMPANIMENTS Pour lemon juice over the banana to prevent discolouration. Cut the palm leaves into rectangles and fold into cones. Secure with toothpicks. Fill each cone with an accompaniment. TO SERVE Pour the chocolate mixture into a little clay pot and place the pot over a low flame. Display the accompaniments around.

WINE 1997 Allesverloren Estate Port, Swartland, South Africa

Soneva Gili, located on the island of Lankanfushi, is a short 15-minute boat ride from Malé.
OPPOSITE (FROM TOP): Hot chocolate soufflé with mango and mint ice cream; Stuffed white cabbage leaves and crispy tofu with wasabi-sake sauce; Green asparagus velouté with white truffle oil and tomato tartare.

GREEN ASPARAGUS VELOUTE WITH WHITE TRUFFLE OIL & TOMATO TARTARE Serves 2

GREEN ASPARAGUS VELOUTE
160 g / 5⅝ oz onions, peeled and chopped
4 cloves garlic, peeled and chopped
100 ml / 3⅜ fl oz / ⅜ cup olive oil
1 L / 1 pt 15 fl oz / 4¼ cups chicken stock (see Basics)
800 g / 1 lb 12¼ oz green asparagus, trimmed and cut into 2-cm / 0.75-inch lengths
200 ml / 6¾ fl oz / ⅞ cup whipping cream
Salt and pepper to taste
TOMATO TARTARE
160 g / 5⅝ oz tomatoes, peeled, seeds and pulp removed and diced
2 sprigs dill, chopped
2 sprigs basil, chopped
2 sprigs parsley, chopped
2 tsp vinegar
1 tsp sugar
½ tsp salt
4 tsp sesame oil
1 tsp white truffle oil for garnishing
4 sprigs chives, chopped for garnishing
A few sprigs of fresh herbs for garnishing

GREEN ASPARAGUS VELOUTE In a pan, sauté the onions and garlic in olive oil until the onions turn translucent. Add the chicken stock, bring to a boil, then add the asparagus and cook until they soften. Add the cream and simmer for 2 minutes. Process the mixture in a blender until smooth, then strain. Season with salt and pepper. TOMATO TARTARE Mix the tomatoes with dill, basil, parsley, vinegar, sugar, salt and sesame oil. TO SERVE Ladle the soup into bowls and sprinkle a few drops of white truffle oil and chopped chives over. On a side plate, present the tomato tartare garnished with fresh herbs.

WINE 2000 Freie Weingärtner Grüner Veltliner Achleiten Smaragd, Wachau, Austria

STUFFED WHITE CABBAGE LEAVES & CRISPY TOFU WITH WASABI-SAKE SAUCE Serves 2

VEGETABLE STUFFING
60 g / 2⅛ oz green beans
60 g / 2⅛ oz green asparagus
2 cloves garlic, peeled and chopped
1 sprig spring onions, peeled and chopped
100 g / 3½ oz carrot, cut into sticks
60 g / 2⅛ oz baby corn, halved
60 g / 2⅛ oz snow peas, cut into thin strips
60 g / 2⅛ oz red capsicum, seeds removed and cut into thin strips
4 tsp vegetable oil
2 tsp oyster sauce
4 tsp light soy sauce
4 sprigs coriander, chopped
WHITE CABBAGE LEAF WRAP
2 big (or 4 small) white cabbage leaves, trimmed
2 green leek leaves
WASABI-SAKE SAUCE
4 tsp sake
2 tsp sugar
2 tsp wasabi
2 tsp coconut milk
4 tsp sesame oil
CRISPY TOFU
30 g / 1 oz tofu for frying, cut into cubes
5 tsp cornstarch
Vegetable oil for pan-frying
A few sprigs of fresh herbs for garnishing

VEGETABLE STUFFING Blanch the green beans and asparagus in boiling salted water until they soften, then refresh with iced water. In a wok, sauté the garlic, spring onions and all the vegetables, including the beans and asparagus, in the vegetable oil until cooked. Add the oyster sauce, soy sauce and coriander and toss well. WHITE CABBAGE LEAF WRAP Blanch the cabbage and leek leaves in boiling salted water until they soften, then refresh with iced water. Place a portion of stuffing in the middle of each cabbage leaf and wrap the leaf neatly around it. Tie the parcel with the leek leaf and steam for 5 minutes. WASABI-SAKE SAUCE Boil the sake with the sugar. Add the wasabi, mix well, then add the coconut milk and boil for 1 minute. Remove from heat and blend in the sesame oil. CRISPY TOFU Roll the tofu cubes in cornstarch and pan-fry until they just begin to brown. TO SERVE Place a stuffed cabbage leaf in the centre of a plate and drizzle the sauce around. Garnish with crispy tofu and sprigs of fresh herbs.

WINE 2000 Château Fortia Châteauneuf-du-Pape Blanc, Rhône, France

HOT CHOCOLATE SOUFFLE WITH MANGO & MINT ICE CREAM Serves 2

HOT CHOCOLATE SOUFFLE
100 g / 3½ oz dark chocolate, cracked
1½ tsp milk
1½ tsp water
50 g / 1¾ oz / ¼ cup sugar
1½ egg yolks
1½ egg whites, whisked until stiff
A pinch of salt
1 tsp butter for greasing soufflé moulds
MANGO & MINT ICE CREAM
500 ml / 17½ fl oz / 2⅛ cups milk
4 egg yolks
100 g / 3½ oz / ½ cup sugar
400 g / 14⅛ oz mangoes, peeled, seeds removed
and flesh puréed
200 ml / 6¾ fl oz / ⅞ cups whipping cream
4 sprigs mint, chopped
1 tsp icing sugar for dusting
2 sprigs mint leaves for garnishing

HOT CHOCOLATE SOUFFLE Preheat the oven to 180°C / 350°F. Melt half the dark chocolate in a bain marie and whisk in the milk, water and half the sugar until smooth. Remove from heat and whisk in the egg yolks and whites, salt, remaining chocolate and sugar until well incorporated. Pour the chocolate mixture into 2 buttered soufflé moulds and bake for 13 minutes. MANGO & MINT ICE CREAM Bring the milk to a simmer. Beat the egg yolks and sugar until white and fluffy. Add the hot milk and cook over low heat, stirring constantly. When it starts to thicken, remove from heat and set aside to cool. When cool, add the mango purée, cream and chopped mint, mix well and pour the mixture into an ice cream machine. Follow the manufacturer's directions. TO SERVE Dust the soufflé with icing sugar and serve with a scoop of mango and mint ice cream garnished with mint leaves on the side.

WINE 1998 Weingut Dr Heger Spätbürgunder Beerenauslese, Ihringer Winklerberg, Baden, Germany

GAZPACHO WITH STEAMED CRAYFISH MEDALLIONS Serves 2

GAZPACHO
1 kg / 2 lbs 3¼ oz tomatoes, halved
50 g / 1¾ oz onions, peeled and quartered
60 g / 2⅛ oz red capsicum, seeds removed and halved
80 g / 2⅞ oz cucumber, peeled and seeds removed
5 tsp olive oil
50 g / 1¾ oz bread, all crusts removed
50 ml / 1¾ fl oz / ¼ cup milk
1 tsp mustard
1 clove garlic, peeled and crushed
2 sprigs basil
100 ml / 3⅜ fl oz / ⅜ cup chicken stock (see Basics)
1 tsp sugar
1 tsp ketchup
½ tsp tomato paste
5 tsp vinegar
Salt and pepper to taste
Tabasco sauce to taste
2 tsp mayonnaise
STEAMED CRAYFISH MEDALLIONS
200 g / 7 oz crayfish tails
Salt and pepper to taste
A few drops of olive oil for garnishing

GAZPACHO Preheat the oven to 180°C /350°F. Brush the tomatoes, onions, capsicum and cucumber with olive oil and place them on a greased oven tray. Roast for 35 minutes. In the meantime, soak the bread in milk. Combine this, the roasted vegetables and the mustard, garlic, basil, chicken stock, sugar, ketchup and tomato paste in a large bowl to marinate for 24 hours. Keep refrigerated during this time. Process the mixture in a blender until smooth. Season with vinegar, salt, pepper, Tabasco sauce and mayonnaise, then strain and chill. STEAMED CRAYFISH MEDALLIONS Season the crayfish with salt and pepper and steam until it just turns bright orange. Let cool, then cut the tail in half lengthwise, remove the shell and slice the meat into medallions. Skewer the medallions. TO SERVE Pour the chilled soup into 4 bowls or 8 to 10 shooter glasses and garnish each with a few drops of olive oil. Serve with the crayfish skewers.

WINE 2002 Castello della Sala Chardonnay, IGT Umbria Antinori, Italy

PAPILLOTE OF REEF FISH & VEGETABLE TAGLIATELLE WITH LEMON OIL & FRESH HERB PESTO Serves 2

PAPILLOTE OF REEF FISH
4 tsp olive oil
1 tsp salt
4 tsp whole black peppercorns
1 tsp chopped lime rind
1 tsp chopped lemon rind
2 (each about 150 g / 5¼ oz) white snapper or sole fillets
2 lime leaves
VEGETABLE TAGLIATELLE
160 g / 5⅝ oz carrots
100 g / 3½ oz yellow zucchini
100 g / 3½ oz green zucchini
2 tsp lemon oil
FRESH HERB PESTO
40 g / 1⅜ oz / ¼ cup pine nuts
6 sprigs sweet basil
100 ml / 3⅜ fl oz / ⅜ cup olive oil
4 tsp balsamic vinegar
½ tsp salt
SALAD
4 rocket leaves
6 mizuna leaves
4 lollo rosso leaves
2 radicchio leaves
2 sprigs mint leaves
DRESSING
4 tsp lime juice
4 tbsp olive oil
Salt and white pepper powder to taste
2 lime wedges for garnishing
A few sprigs of fresh herbs for garnishing

PAPILLOTE OF REEF FISH Preheat the oven to 160°C / 320°F. Mix the olive oil with salt, pepper, lime and lemon rind. Roll the fish in it. With greaseproof paper, fold 2 boxes large enough to hold a portion of fish. Put the fish in, cover each with a lime leaf and cover the box. Bake the papillote in the oven for 15 minutes. VEGETABLE TAGLIATELLE Using a mandolin, slice the carrots and zucchinis into thin strips. Mix with lemon oil and salt to taste. Steam for 2 minutes. FRESH HERB PESTO Process the pine nuts in a blender until powdery. Add the basil leaves and process until roughly mixed. Slowly add the olive oil, balsamic vinegar and salt and process until smooth (but avoid over-blending or the basil leaves will lose their colour). SALAD Mix the salad leaves with mint leaves. DRESSING Whisk the lime juice, olive oil, salt and pepper until well mixed. TO SERVE Toss the salad in the dressing then divide the salad, vegetable tagliatelle and papillote between 2 plates and pour some pesto over the tagliatelle. Garnish each serving with a wedge of lime and fresh herbs.

WINE 2000 Bannockburn Geelong Chardonnay, Victoria, Australia

RED WILD FOREST FRUIT SOUP WITH SWEET BLACK OLIVES & YOGHURT SORBET Serves 2

RED WILD FOREST FRUIT SOUP
250 ml / 8½ fl oz / 1 cup red wine (pinot noir)
250 ml / 8½ fl oz / 1 cup water
150 g / 5¼ oz / ¾ cup sugar
3 vanilla pods, halved lengthwise
80 g / 2⅞ oz pitted cherries
80 g / 2⅞ oz strawberries
80 g / 2⅞ oz blueberries
50 g / 1¾ oz raspberries
SWEET BLACK OLIVES
30 g / 1 oz pitted black olives, sliced thinly
100 ml / 3⅜ fl oz / ⅜ cup water
50 g / 1¾ oz / ¼ cup sugar
YOGHURT SORBET
120 g / 4¼ oz / ⅔ cup sugar
500 ml / 17 fl oz / 2⅛ cups milk
500 g / 1 lb 1⅝ oz yoghurt
250 ml / 8½ fl oz / 1 cup whipping cream
2 sprigs mint for garnishing

RED WILD FOREST FRUIT SOUP In a pot, combine the red wine, water, sugar and vanilla pods and boil for 10 minutes. Reduce the heat and add the cherries and strawberries. Continue cooking for 10 minutes before adding the blueberries and raspberries, then cook for a further 5 minutes. When cool, chill overnight. Reserve vanilla pods for garnishing. SWEET BLACK OLIVES Blanch the olives in boiling water for 10 minutes to remove the taste of salt. Boil the water and sugar to make a syrup. Add the olives and simmer for 20 minutes. Let the olives sit in the syrup overnight. YOGHURT SORBET Boil the sugar and milk, and mix in the yoghurt and cream. Pour the mixture into an ice cream machine. Follow the manufacturer's directions to prepare a sorbet. TO SERVE Pour the soup into 2 bowls and place a scoop of sorbet in the middle of each. Sprinkle the olives around and garnish with the vanilla pods and mint sprigs.

WINE 1999 Pettental Riesling Auslese, Rheinhessen, Germany

Gazpacho with steamed crayfish medallions. OPPOSITE (FROM TOP): Red wild forest fruit soup with sweet black olives and yoghurt sorbet; Papillote of reef fish and vegetable tagliatelle with lemon oil and fresh herb pesto.

AS RECENTLY AS 15 years ago, Koh Samui was considered a little piece of hippie heaven. The tiny island was paradise for backpackers trying to escape the flashy bars and clubs of Pattaya and the increasingly popular Phuket beaches. Throughout most of the 1970s and even into the early 1980s, the majority of places to stay on this small island were little more than beach shacks. Many were as cheap as US$6 a day. For that price, you would probably get a roof over your head and maybe, if you were lucky, a shower that worked. But that was it. Fortunately, that was just fine for most of the people who came at that time. These travellers were here for the sun and the sand, and not much else. And they also knew that the views from their ramshackle little bungalows were worth far more than what they were paying.

It was only a matter of time, however, before significant development began making inroads upon the island, and over the past few years, larger resorts have opened, with extensive modern facilities and services. Newer restaurants and shops have followed, along with an ever-increasing number of visitors. The significant rise in arrivals has forced Samui's authorities to consider the issue of tourism very carefully. Fortunately for the island's 40,000 inhabitants, tourism was not, and still is not, their main source of income. Samui's inland hill areas are home to lucrative coconut and rubber farming industries. Samui, it might be noted, has more varieties of coconut palms than anywhere else in the world, and is sometimes referred to as the world's coconut capital.

Much to its credit, Samui's government took a two-pronged approach towards tourism in the late 1990s. Firstly, it set up very specific restrictions on construction in order to preserve the island's natural environment. Forests, beaches and the sea were to be protected. Having seen what chaos unplanned building had inflicted upon some other Thai islands, the people of Samui were only being wise.

Secondly, in 1999, Samui initiated an island-wide effort to upgrade its infrastructure. Roads were paved and widened. Drainage systems were fixed and sidewalks were created in the popular villages of Chaweng and Laweng. Visitors who had come prior to 1999 were amazed by the transformation that the island was undergoing.

The most recent phase of this remarkable metamorphosis has been the development of the luxury hotel market on Samui. While the island had seen a boom in resorts throughout the 1990s, the majority of these were built to appeal to backpackers and mid-range travellers. In 2000, you could count the number of top-end hotels on the island on one hand. Now, however, travel trade magazines are constantly abuzz with rumours about which of the world's greatest resort brands are setting up camp in this former hippie enclave.

One such resort is Evason's new, exclusive all-villa retreat, located on the cape of Samrong Bay at the northern tip of the island. Sila Evason Hideaway & Spa is set amongst

The inviting glow from a villa is a welcoming sight after a long day at the beach.
OPPOSITE: A combination of organic materials and modern lines makes up the 66 villas in Sila Evason Hideaway & Spa at Samui.

approximately eight hectares (20 acres) of indigenous foliage, with spectacular views of the sea and outlying islands. The resort comprises 66 two-level villas, and 52 of these have their own infinity-edged private swimming pools. The smallest of the villas is a very comfortable 130 square metres (approximately 1,400 square feet) in area.

Design buffs will love staying here. The villas can only be described as 'modern tropical', with clean lines and light, airy spaces. The colour scheme here is brown and white. Natural wood provides most of the rich brown tones, while light tones are reflected everywhere, from the soft furnishings to the wall textures.

Sila Evason Hideaway offers a select range of services. If you really feel the need to leave your villa—despite having your own personal butler on call 24 hours a day—we suggest taking advantage of the excellent therapies provided at the Spa, a sure way to stay relaxed even outside your villa. The Spa has both indoor and outdoor treatment rooms for individuals and couples. The resort also has an excellent water sports centre and a huge central infinity-edged pool.

Gourmands will fully appreciate the food at Sila Evason Hideaway, where guests have two restaurants to choose from. The resort's main restaurant sits atop a small hill and overlooks the sea towards the north. The more formal restaurant is located at the tip of the headland, and offers 270-degree views of the sea and surrounding islands. The food at both restaurants also matches the stunning scenery, with a range of menus available which offers Thai, international, healthy spa specialities and, of course, the fusion cuisine that has made all the Six Senses resorts famous among epicures from all around the world.

Sila Evason Hideaway & Spa, with its modern, luxurious villas, perfectly attentive service and exceptional food, is definitely a little piece of heaven on earth. Only these days, it's decidedly not just for hippies.

TIAN OF LAMB LOIN WITH GRILLED MEDITERRANEAN VEGETABLES & GOAT CHEESE Serves 8

TIAN OF LAMB LOIN
60 g / 2⅛ oz lamb loin
4 cloves garlic, peeled and chopped
Salt and pepper to taste
200 g / 7 oz clarified butter
GRILLED MEDITERRANEAN VEGETABLES
200 g / 7 oz whole red capsicum
200 g / 7 oz whole yellow capsicum
200 g / 7 oz whole green capsicum
200 g / 7 oz tomatoes, skin removed
240 g / 8½ oz artichokes
Extra virgin olive oil for marinating
1 tbsp chopped garlic
1 tbsp chopped rosemary
1 tbsp chopped thyme
1 tsp chopped chilli
300 g / 10½ oz goat cheese, sliced
200 g / 7 oz beetroot, cut into thin strips and deep-fried for garnishing
8 sprigs of deep-fried rosemary for garnishing

TIAN OF LAMB LOIN Preheat oven to 180°C / 350°F. Rub the lamb loin with garlic, salt and pepper. Sauté the lamb in a little clarified butter. Once the lamb is browned on all sides, place it in the oven for 2 to 3 minutes for medium-rare or until desired doneness. Let it rest for 10 to 15 minutes in a warm place, about 50 to 60°C / 120 to 140°F, before slicing. GRILLED MEDITERRANEAN VEGETABLES Marinate the whole vegetables in extra virgin olive oil with garlic, rosemary, thyme and chilli, and grill for about 20 minutes or until slightly blackened. Let cool, then cut into slices. TO SERVE Layer the vegetables, goat cheese and lamb loin on a fork or skewer. Garnish with a little deep-fried beetroot and rosemary.

WINE 1989 Rioja Cincel, Gran Reserva, Spain

LOBSTER TAIL COCKTAIL WITH APPLE-LIME LEAF COMPOTE & TOM YAM SORBET Serves 8

LOBSTER TAIL COCKTAIL
100 g / 3½ oz lemon grass, chopped
100 g / 3½ oz galangal, chopped
12 lime leaves, chopped
20 g / ¾ oz coriander, chopped
4 lobster tails, shells removed
APPLE-LIME LEAF COMPOTE
200 g / 7 oz apples, peeled and cut in chunks
5 lime leaves, cut into thin strips
4 tsp sugar
TOM YAM SORBET
200 ml / 6¾ fl oz / ⅞ cup sugar syrup (dissolve 2 parts sugar in 1 part water)
700 ml / 1 pt 4½ fl oz / 3 cups water
Juice from 2 limes
40 g / 1⅜ oz lemon grass, chopped
5 lime leaves, torn into pieces
2 tbsp fish sauce
50 g / 1¾ oz mushrooms, cut into wedges
3 chillies, chopped
120 g / 4¼ oz red onion, peeled and chopped
30 g / 1 oz galangal, chopped
140 g / 5 oz tomato, chopped into chunks
2 stalks coriander, chopped
3 tbsp wasabi mayonnaise (see Basics)
60 g / 2⅛ oz iceberg lettuce
Salt and pepper to taste

LOBSTER TAIL COCKTAIL Preheat oven to 180°C / 350°F. Mix the chopped lemon grass, galangal, lime leaf and coriander. Roll the lobster tail in the mixture and sauté in hot olive oil until the crust holds. Finish cooking by baking for 3 to 4 minutes. When done, season the lobster with salt and pepper. Keep warm. APPLE-LIME LEAF COMPOTE Mix all the ingredients together in a small pan and simmer for 15 to 18 minutes until cooked. Chill. TOM YAM SORBET Mix all the ingredients together and bring to a boil. Remove from heat and let stand for 20 minutes. Strain the mixture and process it in an ice cream machine according to manufacturer's instructions. Keep frozen until required. TO SERVE Cut 2 generous slices of warm lobster and stick them on a fork or skewer. Drizzle a little wasabi mayonnaise on the lobster and stack a little iceberg lettuce on the top. Place the chilled apple compôte on top of the lettuce and some frozen sorbet on top of that. Serve immediately.

WINE 2003 Echeverria, Sauvignon Blanc, Molina, Chile

BLACKENED PRAWNS WITH SPICY MANGO Serves 8

BLACKENED PRAWNS
16 jumbo prawns, shells and veins removed but with tails intact
200 ml / 6¾ fl oz / ⅞ cup Thai spicy sweet chilli sauce
8 cloves garlic, peeled and chopped
20 g / ¾ oz coriander leaves, chopped
4 stalks lemon grass, chopped
4 tsp olive oil
SPICY MANGO
4 ripe yellow Alfonzo mangoes, peeled and cut into large cubes
4 chillies, chopped
20 g / ¾ oz coriander leaves, chopped
Coriander leaves for garnishing

BLACKENED PRAWNS Marinate the prawns in the Thai chilli sauce with garlic, coriander leaves and lemon grass overnight. When ready, blacken the prawns in a very hot non-stick pan with olive oil for about 3 minutes until they are cooked medium-well. Let rest for 5 minutes. SPICY MANGO Mix the mango cubes with the chopped chilli and coriander. TO SERVE Slice the blackened prawns into medallions. Layer them on a fork or skewer topped with cubes of mango. Garnish with coriander leaves.

WINE 2000 Trilogy, Collio Bianco, Fantinel, Italy

Extending over the waters, the sharp lines of the poolside pavilion create a striking contrast against the expansive, scenic backdrop.
OPPOSITE (FROM LEFT): Tian of lamb loin with grilled Mediterranean vegetables and goat cheese; Lobster tail cocktail with apple-lime leaf compôte and tom yam sorbet; Blackened prawns with spicy mango.

SEARED PRAWNS & SCALLOPS WITH CELERIAC PUREE, CANDIED ORANGE ZEST & AROMATIC OIL Serves 2

AROMATIC OIL
5 tbsp chopped scallions, basil and coriander
80 ml / 2¾ oz / ⅓ cup grapeseed oil
Salt to taste
LOBSTER OIL
6 cloves garlic
1 stalk rosemary
5 stalks thyme
350 ml / 11⅞ fl oz / 1½ cups olive oil
500 g / 1 lb 1⅝ oz lobster shells, cut into small chunks
1 tsp paprika powder
3 tbsp tomato purée
CANDIED ORANGE ZEST
280 ml / 9⅓ fl oz / 1⅛ cups water
5 tbsp sugar
Orange zest (orange part only) from 2 oranges
CELERIAC PUREE
500 g / 1 lb 1⅝ oz celeriac, peeled and cut into chunks
Celery salt to taste
50 to 100 ml / 2 to 3⅜ fl oz / ¼ to ⅜ cup heavy cream
SEARED PRAWNS & SCALLOPS
6 (280 g / 9¾ oz) tiger prawns, shells and vein removed but with tail intact
6 scallops, shells removed
100 ml / 3⅜ fl oz / ⅜ cup olive oil
3 tbsp demi-glace (see Basics)
50 ml / 1¾ fl oz / ¼ cup
2 crispy potato wafers (see Basics)

AROMATIC OIL Mix the herbs with grapeseed oil and purée in a blender. Season with salt and refrigerate for 4 hours to thicken. LOBSTER OIL Simmer garlic, rosemary and thyme in a little oil over medium heat. Once the aromas are released, add the lobster shells. Increase the heat and stir constantly to ensure the lobster shells turn red. First add the paprika, then the tomato purée. Continue to stir to ensure the paprika is mixed well. When the tomato purée turns slightly brown, add the remaining oil until the lobster shells are covered under it. Let it simmer on a low flame, reaching about 80 to 90°C / 175 to 195°F to drive out any water but not burn the ingredients. Once this has reduced by half, strain and store the oil ready for use. CANDIED ORANGE ZEST Preheat oven to a 190°C / 375°F. Heat the water and dissolve the sugar in it. Add the zest and bring to a boil. Then lower the heat and reduce the mixture until all orange zest is glazed in a thick syrupy mass. Remove the zest from the pan and set it on an oven rack or roasting tray. Lay another rack on top of it and dry the zest in the oven for 20 minutes. Let cool and crush it in a mortar. Store in an airtight box away from humidity. CELERIAC PUREE Boil the celeriac until well done and drain. Allow remaining water to evaporate by heating without covering for 2 minutes, all the while moving the celeriac every few seconds so it does not stick. Purée the celeriac in a blender. Add the celery salt to taste. Blend the purée with some heavy cream to get a soft and smooth purée, taking care not add too much as the purée should be stiff, not runny. Push the purée through a fine sieve to remove all chunks and get a smooth purée. SEARED PRAWNS & SCALLOPS In a pan, sauté the prawns and scallops with 1 tbsp of olive oil at high temperature to seal the prawns. When medium-well done, remove to an oven tray. TO SERVE Warm the demi-glace, and keep ready. Warm the prawns and scallops quickly in a hot oven at 230°C / 450°F, and re-heat the potato wafers for 30 seconds in the oven. Place a portion of the celeriac purée in the centre of each serving plate. Place the prawns and scallops on it, leaning against each other. Put a thin layer of the celeriac purée on top of the prawns and scallops and top with a potato wafer. Drizzle the aromatic oil, demi-glace and lobster oil around the dish. Garnish with a sprinkling of candied orange zest.

WINE 2001 Buitenverwachting Sauvignon Blanc, Constantia, South Africa

Seared prawns and scallops with celeriac purée, candied orange zest and aromatic oil.
OPPOSITE: Curried lobster tail, soft potato rouille with cumin-crusted filo pastry and artichoke salad.

CURRIED LOBSTER TAIL, SOFT POTATO ROUILLE WITH CUMIN-CRUSTED FILO PASTRY & ARTICHOKE SALAD Serves 2

CURRIED LOBSTER TAIL
700 g to 1 kg / 1 lb 8⅝ oz to 2 lb 3¼ oz lobster
30 g / 1 oz / ¼ cup Madras curry powder
Oil for frying
100 g / 3½ oz red onion, peeled and wedged
3 cloves garlic, peeled and chopped
200 ml / 6¾ fl oz / ⅞ cup chicken stock (see Basics)
100 ml / 3⅜ fl oz / ⅜ cup coconut milk
1 tbsp oyster sauce
1 large chilli
60 g / 2⅛ oz spring onion, chopped
POTATO ROUILLE
2 to 3 tsp garlic purée
2 to 3 tbsp extra virgin olive oil
A pinch of saffron
200 g / 7 oz potato purée
Salt and pepper to taste
ARTICHOKE SALAD
2 medium artichokes, cooked and quartered
100 g / 3½ oz haricot vert (French beans)
50 g / 1¾ oz frisée
1 handful shallots, peeled and finely chopped
3 tbsp lobster oil (see previous recipe)
100 g / 3½ oz fresh spinach
Cumin-crusted filo pastry (see Basics)
½ tsp chopped garlic
Oil for frying
Coriander leaves for garnishing

CURRIED LOBSTER TAIL Carefully remove the lobster meat in 1 piece from the shell. Dice it into large chunks. In a wok, fry the curry powder with a little oil. Add the red onion and garlic. Fry, stirring constantly, and add the lobster when the onion turns translucent. Once the lobster is well covered with curry and half cooked, add chicken stock and reduce the heat. Add the coconut milk, oyster sauce, chilli and spring onion, and cook the lobster on low heat until done. Season to taste. POTATO ROUILLE Sauté the garlic purée in a little olive oil. Add the saffron and simmer for 3 to 4 minutes, stirring constantly. Once the garlic has dissolved and the colour of the saffron has been released, add the potato purée. Mix well and heat through. Add enough olive oil to get a rich and smooth texture. Keep warm. ARTICHOKE SALAD Toss all ingredients well in 2 tbsp lobster oil. TO SERVE Sauté the spinach with the garlic in a little oil. Place some warm potato rouille on a sheet of cumin-crusted pastry. Pile on a portion of curried lobster, sautéed spinach and artichoke salad. Top with another sheet of pastry. Repeat this twice more to create a small tower. Top with a coriander sprig. Drizzle with lobster oil and curry sauce from the pan.

WINE 2000 Enate Barrique Fermented Chardonnay, Somontano, Spain

BROILED SALMON IN MISO SAUCE WITH CRISPY BITTER VEGETABLES, JAPANESE MUSHROOMS & SOBA Serves 2

MISO SAUCE
4 tbsp dark miso
2 tbsp honey
1 tbsp Japanese peanut paste
2 tbsp teriyaki sauce
BROILED SALMON
450 g / 15⅞ oz salmon fillet, skin removed and cut into 2 portions
Sea salt to taste
BLACK OLIVE EMULSION
75 g / 2⅝ oz / ⅔ cup black olives, dried and ground
200 ml / 6¾ fl oz / ⅞ cup extra virgin olive oil
CRISPY BITTER VEGETABLES, JAPANESE MUSHROOMS & SOBA
125 g / 4 oz / 1¼ cups Japanese green noodles
100 g / 3½ oz beetroot, leek and zucchini, cut into sticks
80 g / 2⅞ oz witlof, cut into thin slices
80 g / 2⅞ oz shiitake mushrooms, sliced
80 g / 2⅞ oz enoki mushrooms
100 ml / 3⅜ fl oz / ⅜ cup black olive emulsion
A few drops of truffle oil

MISO SAUCE Mix all the ingredients well. BROILED SALMON Marinate the salmon fillets in the miso sauce. Cover tightly and set aside in the refrigerator for 2 days. Every 6 hours, turn the salmon over and stir the marinade. Sauté the salmon fillets in hot oil and add a little of the marinade while frying. Keep moving the salmon in the pan to prevent it from sticking and burning. When the salmon is medium-well done and caramelised, remove it from the pan. Season with a little sea salt and cover with aluminium foil. Set aside and keep warm. BLACK OLIVE EMULSION Mix the ground olives with the extra virgin olive oil. Strain the mixture through a very fine sieve. Reserve the black olive oil for use. (If desired, the leftover purée can be dried again and used as a garnishing powder in other dishes.) CRISPY BITTER VEGETABLES, JAPANESE MUSHROOMS & SOBA Boil the noodles and deep-fry the vegetable sticks. Deep-fry a small amount of soba for garnishing and season with salt. Sauté the witlof and mushrooms at a high temperature. Season with salt and pepper. TO SERVE Roll the noodles on a fork and slide them off in the middle of a serving plate. Place the salmon on that. Set the sautéed mushrooms on the salmon. Top it with the crispy vegetables and fried soba. Drizzle the black olive emulsion around it and garnish with a few drops of truffle oil.

WINE 2000 Iphöfer Kronsberg Silvaner Spätlese, Franken, Germany

The placid waters of the Gulf Stream complement the serene atmosphere in the restaurant.
OPPOSITE (FROM TOP): Broiled salmon in miso sauce with crispy bitter vegetables, Japanese mushrooms and soba; Jasmine tea-flavoured chocolate pots with spiced pineapple.

JASMINE TEA-FLAVOURED CHOCOLATE POTS WITH SPICED PINEAPPLE Serves 2

JASMINE TEA-FLAVOURED CHOCOLATE POTS
120 ml / 4 fl oz / ½ cup whipping cream
½ tsp jasmine tea
A pinch of nutmeg
40 g / 1⅜ oz dark bitter chocolate, grated
SPICED PINEAPPLE
4 tsp water
3½ tbsp sugar
2 very thin, round slices of pineapple
½ tsp five spice powder
2 sprigs of mint for garnishing

JASMINE TEA-FLAVOURED CHOCOLATE POTS Combine cream, tea and nutmeg in a saucepan and bring to a boil. Remove from heat and let infuse for 5 minutes. Put the chocolate in a bowl set in a pan of hot water and strain the mixture over it. Stir until the chocolate dissolves. Pour it into espresso cups and refrigerate for at least 3 hours. SPICED PINEAPPLE Warm the water and dissolve the sugar in it to make a syrup. Drench the slices of pineapple in the syrup. Put them on an oven tray lined with baking paper and sprinkle with the five spice powder. Place an oven rack on top of the chips to prevent them from curling as they dry in an oven at 60°C / 140°F for 10 to 12 hours, or until crispy. Store the chips in an airtight container until ready to use. TO SERVE Serve the chocolate pots straight from the fridge, topped with pineapple chips and garnished with mint.

WINE 1999 Inniskillin Gold Label Oak Aged Vidal Icewine, Okanagan, Canada

SAFFRON-WHITE & FIVE SPICE-DARK CHOCOLATE MOUSSE CONE Serves 2

SAFFRON-WHITE CHOCOLATE MOUSSE
7 tsp milk
A pinch of saffron
340 g / 12 oz white chocolate
5½ tbsp sugar
8 egg yolks
250 ml / 8½ fl oz / 1 cup whipping cream
2 egg whites
FIVE SPICE-DARK CHOCOLATE MOUSSE
2 tsp five spice powder
5 tbsp milk
600 g / 2⅛ oz unsweetened dark chocolate
6 tbsp sugar
12 eggs
2 marbled chocolate cones
20 amarena cherries

SAFFRON-WHITE CHOCOLATE MOUSSE
Bring the milk and saffron to a boil. When almost boiling, reduce the heat and maintain a temperature of about 70°C / 160°F for 5 minutes to allow the saffron to release its colour. Set aside. Melt the white chocolate in a bain marie and maintain it at around 35 to 40°C / 95 to 105°F. Meanwhile, mix 70 percent of the sugar with the egg yolks and beat until foamy. Whip the cream to a heavy syrup thickness. Using a clean bowl and whisk, beat the egg whites until they start to turn white. Then add the remaining sugar and continue whipping until the whites are foamy and stiff. Now whisk the yolk mixture and the white chocolate together. Then, using a spatula, fold in the saffron-milk mixture, followed by the whipping cream and the egg whites. Fold in with the spatula as quickly yet gently as possible, preserving as much air as possible in the mixture. Put the mousse in a plastic container and store in the refrigerator. FIVE SPICE-DARK CHOCOLATE MOUSSE Mix the five spice powder with the milk and heat it to 80°C / 175°F. Set aside the let the spice powder infuse the milk. Meanwhile, melt the dark chocolate and maintain it at around 35 to 40°C / 95 to 105°F. Beat the eggs with the sugar in a bain marie until foamy. Mix the milk mixture with the chocolate. Using a spatula, fold in the eggs immediately afterwards, mixing as quickly yet gently as possible. Store in a plastic container in the refrigerator. ASSEMBLY In a chilled environment, fill the marbled chocolate cone with a little dark chocolate mousse. Put a few amarena cherries on top of that. Repeat again with the saffron-white chocolate mousse and chill. TO SERVE Present the cone upright by freezing the tip of the cone into an ice-plate or block.

WINE 1974 Fattoria del Teso, Vin Santo del Teso Riserva, Tuscany, Italy

Perched on a slope, each exclusive villa is discreetly screened by walls of lush foliage and bamboo.
OPPOSITE (FROM LEFT): Saffron-white and five spice-dark chocolate mousse cone; Chermoulah-spiced tiger prawns with avocado-coriander mash; Carpaccio of ahi tuna with red capsicum salsa and caramelised mango.

CHERMOULAH-SPICED TIGER PRAWNS WITH AVOCADO-CORIANDER MASH Serves 2

CHERMOULAH SPICES
50 g / 1¾ oz garlic, peeled and chopped
50 g / 1¾ oz shallot, peeled and chopped
50 g / 1¾ oz cayenne pepper, chopped
10 g / ⅜ oz coriander, chopped
100 ml / 3⅜ fl oz / ⅜ cup olive oil
2 tsp paprika powder
1 tsp cumin powder
4 tsp lemon juice
Salt and pepper to taste
TIGER PRAWNS
6 tiger prawns, shells and veins removed but with tails intact
Oil for frying
AVOCADO-CORIANDER MASH
2 ripe avocados, peeled and seeds removed
1 small onion, peeled and minced
1 clove garlic, peeled and minced
1 small tomato, chopped
1 to 3 small chillies, minced
1½ tbsp lime juice
Salt and pepper to taste
Lettuce leaves (lollo rosso, oakleaf and frisée)
2 sprigs coriander for garnishing
3 tbsp chilli dressing
3 tbsp curry oil

CHERMOULAH SPICES Heat the chopped ingredients in a little olive oil and simmer over medium heat. Mix in the paprika and cumin powders. Add the lemon juice and season with salt and pepper. Add the remaining oil and mix well. Remove from heat and use when cool. TIGER PRAWNS Marinate the prawns in 300 g / 10½ oz of chermoulah spices for 2 days in the refrigerator. Sauté the prawns in hot oil without burning the spices until medium-well done. AVOCADO-CORIANDER MASH Mash the avocado in a bowl and stir in the remaining ingredients. Season with lime juice, salt and pepper. TO SERVE Arrange 3 prawns on each plate and place a serving of avocado-coriander mash on each prawn. Toss the lettuce in a little chilli dressing and heap the leaves on the prawns. Garnish with coriander. Drizzle the spice oil around.

WINE 2000 Weingut Dr. Heger, Muskateller Ihringer Winklerberg, Baden, Germany

CARPACCIO OF AHI TUNA WITH RED CAPSICUM SALSA & CARAMELISED MANGO
Serves 2

CARPACCIO OF AHI TUNA
200 g / 7 oz fillet of ahi tuna or yellow or blue fin tuna
RED CAPSICUM SALSA
1 red capsicum
1 tbsp mirin
3 to 4 tsp extra virgin olive oil
Honey to taste
CARAMELISED MANGO
1 tbsp honey
200 g / 7 oz mango, finely diced
100 ml / 3⅜ fl oz / ⅜ cup wasabi mayonnaise (see Basics)
4 tsp truffle oil
A few coriander leaves for garnishing
Salt and pepper to taste

CARPACCIO OF AHI TUNA Use cling film to roll the tuna fillet tightly into a cylinder and twist the ends to compact the fish. Place the cylinder in the freezer until it is nearly frozen. Do not let it freeze, as this will destroy the texture. With a very sharp knife, slice the tuna very thinly. Place each slice clockwise on a serving plate. Avoid overlapping the slices. RED CAPSICUM SALSA Roast the red capsicum over an open flame or grill until it blackens slightly. Then cold smoke the capsicum for 15 minutes over hickory wood-chips. Remove the skin and marinate the capsicum with the mirin. Next, process the capsicum in a food processor to a smooth purée and blend in the extra virgin olive oil. If desired, sweeten the salsa with a little honey. CARAMELISED MANGO In a sauté pan heat a little honey and quickly sauté the diced mango. Remove immediately from the pan without letting the mango cook. TO SERVE Drizzle the wasabi mayonnaise and red capsicum salsa across the tuna carpaccio, then sprinkle the caramelised mango, truffle oil and coriander leaves over. Season with a sprinkling of milled salt and pepper.

WINE 2002 Hugel Gewürztraminer Selection de Grains Nobles, Alsace, France

Wide open spaces are an integral part of the design, which seeks to merge the resort with the natural environment; Seared lemon grass and lime leaf-crusted wahoo with rosehip sorbet and apricot compôte.
OPPOSITE (FROM LEFT): Roasted duck breast rolled in goat cheese and pine nuts, with crispy duck and rocket salad; Tian of macerated raspberries and raspberry bavarois.

SEARED LEMON GRASS & LIME LEAF-CRUSTED WAHOO WITH ROSEHIP SORBET & APRICOT COMPOTE Serves 2

ROSEHIP SORBET
200 ml / 6¾ fl oz / ⅞ cup sugar syrup (dissolve 2 parts sugar in 1 part water)
500 ml / 17 fl oz / 2⅛ cups water
1 tbsp rose water
SEARED LEMON GRASS & LIME LEAF-CRUSTED WAHOO
½ tsp wasabi powder
250 g / 8⅞ oz wahoo fillet (or mackerel)
2 stalks lemon grass, chopped finely
10 lime leaves, chopped finely
2 stalks coriander, chopped finely
3 tbsp olive oil
Salt and pepper to taste
APRICOT COMPOTE
2 tbsp honey
200 g / 7 oz dried apricots, cut into thin strips
30 g / 1 oz cinnamon stick
15 g / ½ oz star anise
5 cloves
4 bay leaves
10 whole black peppercorns
250 ml / 8½ fl oz / 1 cup water
BALSAMIC SYRUP
1 L / 1 pt 11 fl oz / 4¼ cups balsamic vinegar
250 g / 8⅞ oz / 1 cup brown sugar
A few mesclun leaves for garnishing
A few sprigs of coriander or thinly sliced lime leaves for garnishing

ROSEHIP SORBET Combine all the ingredients in a bowl and mix well. Process the mixture in an ice cream machine following the manufacturer's instructions. Keep the sorbet frozen until required.

SEARED LEMON GRASS & LIME LEAF-CRUSTED WAHOO Mix the wasabi powder with a little water and rub the mixture on the wahoo fillet. Mix the lemon grass, lime leaves and coriander on a plate and roll the wahoo fillet in this mixture. Heat some oil in a non-stick pan until it starts to smoke, then quickly sear the fillet on all sides for up to 2 minutes, so that the inside remains raw. Remove from heat and season with salt and pepper. Set aside. APRICOT COMPOTE In a saucepan, heat the honey and add the dried apricots. Add all the other ingredients, except the water, and mix well. Caramelise the mixture for about 2 minutes. Deglaze with water and bring to a boil. Lower the heat to a simmer and reduce the mixture to a thick compôte. BALSAMIC SYRUP Combine all the ingredients in a pan and reduce the mixture over medium heat to a third of its original volume. TO SERVE Slice the wahoo thinly. Place a plastic ring about 6 cm / 2.4 inches in diameter in the middle of a plate. Place 3 or 4 slices of the seared wahoo in the ring and on the plate. Top with a layer of apricot compôte followed by the rosehip sorbet. On top of the sorbet, place more slices of wahoo until the top of the sorbet is completely covered. Layer with some more of the apricot compôte and garnish with the mesclun leaves and coriander sprigs or thinly sliced lime leaves. Drizzle a little balsamic syrup around the wahoo and serve immediately.

WINE 1999 Yarden Gewürztraminer, Galilee, Israel

ROASTED DUCK BREAST ROLLED IN GOAT CHEESE & PINE NUTS, WITH CRISPY DUCK & ROCKET SALAD

Serves 2

ROASTED DUCK BREAST ROLLED IN GOAT CHEESE & PINE NUTS
2 duck breasts
Salt and pepper to taste
Oil for frying
150 g / 5¼ oz goat cheese
150 g / 5¼ oz Philadelphia cream cheese
50 g / 1¾ oz / ⅓ cup roasted pine nuts
10 g / ⅜ oz coriander, chopped
CRISPY DUCK & ROCKET SALAD
15 g / ½ oz rocket leaves for garnishing
15 g / ½ oz young salad leaves for garnishing
3 tbsp extra virgin olive oil
1 tbsp balsamic vinegar
250 g / 8⅞ oz large potatoes, cut into 1-by-1-by-12.5-cm / 0.5-by-0.5-by-5-inch sticks
80 g / 2⅞ oz spinach
Olive oil for frying
Salt and pepper to taste
3 tbsp demi-glace (see Basics)
1 tsp orange oil

ROASTED DUCK BREAST ROLLED IN GOAT CHEESE & PINE NUTS Separate the fat from the duck breasts. Season the breasts with salt and pepper and sauté on high heat until caramelised, but with the duck still rare. In the meantime, lay the fat on a roasting pan and place another pan on top to flatten it. Bake at 180°C / 350°F until it becomes golden and crisp, not burnt. Remove from heat and set aside. Slice the breasts thinly and place them like overlapping tiles on a sheet of cling film. In a bowl, mix the goat and cream cheeses with the roasted pine nuts and coriander. Season with salt and pepper. Roll the mixture into a cylinder of similar length as the sliced duck breast on the cling film. Place the cheese roll on the duck slices and roll them tightly into a cylinder. Chill it in the refrigerator at 1°C / 34°F. After 6 to 7 hours, take the roll out and cut it into 2 portions. Set aside. CRISPY DUCK & ROCKET SALAD Slice the crispy baked duck fat into strips and toss well with the rocket, salad leaves, olive oil and balsamic vinegar. TO SERVE Fry the potato in oil heated to 150°C / 300°F for 5 minutes. Set aside. In a hot pan, sauté the spinach with a little olive oil. Season with salt and pepper. Deep-fry the potato again at 180°C / 350°F until golden brown. Season with salt. In a non-stick pan, heat a little olive oil until very hot and quickly sear the duck breast steaks until the cheese has caramelised and the meat is medium done. This has to be done quickly in a very hot pan to avoid overcooking the meat or burning the cheese. Let it rest in a warm place (60°C / 140°F) for 2 minutes. Warm the demi-glace and add the orange oil. Stack the potato sticks in the middle of the plate. Slice the duck breast horizontally into two. Place 1 piece on the potato. Top with some spinach and salad, followed by the other breast. On top of that, place some spinach and finish with more rocket and salad. Garnish with coriander and drizzle the duck-orange sauce around.

WINE 1991 Gaston Hochar Château Musar Red, Bekaa Valley, Lebanon

TIAN OF MACERATED RASPBERRIES & RASPBERRY BAVAROIS Serves 2

MACERATED RASPBERRIES
200 g / 7 oz raspberries
2 tbsp honey
150 ml / 5 fl oz / ⅝ cup crème de cassis
A few drops of crème de menthe
RASPBERRY BAVAROIS
500 ml / 17 fl oz / 2⅛ cup raspberry purée, sweetened
Juice from ½ lemon
13 g / ⅜ oz gelatine powder
250 ml / 8½ fl oz / 1 cup whipping cream
2 to 3 tbsp crème de cassis
2 to 3 tbsp crème de framboise
1 sponge cake, thinly sliced

MACERATED RASPBERRIES Soak the raspberries in the other ingredients for 1 hour. RASPBERRY BAVAROIS Warm the raspberry purée and add lemon juice. Mix the gelatine with a little cold water and dissolve it in the purée. Place the pot in an ice bath to cool the purée. Whip the cream to the consistency of yoghurt and fold it into the purée. Fold in the crème de cassis and crème de framboise. ASSEMBLY Line the inner rings of serving-size ring moulds with sponge cake sprinkled with crème de framboise. Fill a third of the moulds with raspberry bavarois. Top with a layer of macerated raspberries followed by more raspberry bavarois. Refrigerate for 4 hours. TO SERVE Remove moulds to serve.

WINE 2001 De Bortoli, Noble One Botrytis Semillon, Yarra Valley, Australia

Thatched roofs and bamboo details
add to the air of rustic charm.
OPPOSITE: Spiced risotto with roast
chicken, chorizo and ratatouille baked
in claypots.

SPICED RISOTTO WITH ROAST CHICKEN, CHORIZO & RATATOUILLE BAKED IN CLAYPOTS Serves 4

SPICED RISOTTO
40 g / 1¾ oz butter
100 g / 3½ oz shallots, peeled and chopped
400 g / 14⅛ oz / 2 cups arborio rice
400 to 600 ml / 13½ fl oz to 1 pt 1 fl oz / 1⅔ cups to
2 ½ cups chicken stock (see Basics)
ROAST CHICKEN
200 g / 7 oz roasted chicken breast (skin on)
Salt and pepper to taste
Oil for frying
RATATOUILLE
Olive oil for frying
160 g / 5⅝ oz red onion, peeled and finely diced
40 g / 1¾ oz garlic, peeled and chopped
1 tbsp chopped thyme
1 tbsp chopped rosemary
2 tbsp paprika powder
160 g / 5⅝ oz yellow capsicum, finely diced
160 g / 5⅝ oz green capsicum, finely diced
160 g / 5⅝ oz red capsicum, finely diced
240 g / 8½ oz tomato, finely diced
160 g / 5⅝ oz zucchini, finely diced
160 g / 5⅝ oz eggplant, finely diced
A few basil leaves
400 to 600 ml / 13½ fl oz to 1 pt 1 fl oz / 1⅔ cups to
2½ cups tomato pulp
Salt and pepper to taste
200 g / 7 oz chorizo, sliced
Sprigs of basil, thyme and rosemary for garnishing

SPICED RISOTTO Preheat oven to 180°C / 350°F. In an oven-proof dish, heat the butter at a low temperature and fry the shallots until they glaze. Add the rice and fry until the sizzling stops, then add the chicken stock until the rice is covered (about 1.5 cm / 0.8 inch under the broth). Bring to a boil, stir gently and put the lid on the dish. Transfer to the oven and bake for about 25 minutes or until the rice is cooked. When ready, set aside. Meanwhile, maintain the oven at 180°C / 350°F. ROAST CHICKEN Season the chicken breast with salt and pepper. Sauté in a hot pan for 4 to 5 minutes then roast in the oven until medium-well done and the skin is crispy. Set aside in a warm place (60°C / 140°F). RATATOUILLE In a little olive oil, fry the red onion and garlic with a little thyme and rosemary until the aromas rise. Add the paprika powder and fry over medium heat until the powder is incorporated. Add all the vegetables and some basil. Stir-fry again over medium heat. Once the vegetables are glazed, add the tomato pulp, little by little, to the ratatouille. It should not be too wet. Season with salt and pepper to taste. Set aside. ASSEMBLY Fry the chorizo in a little olive oil. Divide among 4 serving-size clay pots, over medium heat. Add the risotto and mix well. Add some of the ratatouille and toss until the rice turns red but is not too wet. Slice the chicken breast and place some sliced chicken on top of the rice. Cover the clay pots and place them in the oven for 8 to 10 minutes to heat through. TO SERVE Garnish the food with some fresh basil, thyme and rosemary and present each person with a claypot.

WINE 1998 Meerlust Rubicon, Stellenbosch, South Africa

Antique taps find their graceful place in the tastefully appointed bathrooms. OPPOSITE: Coconut and truffle froth with roasted artichokes, buckwheat noodles and zucchini mash.

COCONUT & TRUFFLE FROTH WITH ROASTED ARTICHOKES, BUCKWHEAT NOODLES & ZUCCHINI MASH Serves 2

COCONUT & TRUFFLE FROTH
1 tbsp chopped shallots
2 tbsp rosemary oil
200 ml / 6¾ fl oz / ⅞ cup vegetable stock (see Basics)
200 ml / 6¾ fl oz / ⅞ cup coconut milk
4 tsp truffle jus
2 tbsp truffle oil
Salt and pepper to taste

ROASTED ARTICHOKES
2 large artichokes, blanched and outer leaves removed
30 g / 1 oz garlic, peeled and chopped
20 g / ¾ oz rosemary, chopped
2 large chillies, chopped
Extra virgin olive oil for roasting

ZUCCHINI MASH
1 tbsp butter
250 g / 8⅞ oz zucchini, finely grated and soaked in water with a few drops of lemon juice
Salt and pepper to taste

BUCKWHEAT NOODLES
250 g / 8⅞ oz buckwheat noodles
Salt and pepper to taste
A few slices of black truffle for garnishing

COCONUT & TRUFFLE FROTH Fry the shallots in a little rosemary oil over medium heat until glazed. Add the vegetable stock and bring to a boil. Skim off the foam and any material that float to the surface. Reduce the heat and whisk in the coconut milk, adding enough to get a milky colour. Now add the truffle jus and the truffle oil. Put the mixture into a blender and blend well for a minute. Adjust the seasoning. Set aside. ROASTED ARTICHOKES Preheat oven to 180°C / 350°F. Roast the artichokes with garlic, rosemary, chilli and extra virgin olive oil in the oven until they are cooked. Alternatively, they could be grilled or barbecued. Set aside. ZUCCHINI MASH Heat the butter and add the zucchini. Put the lid on the pan to speed up the cooking process. Season with salt and pepper. BUCKWHEAT NOODLES Blanch the noodles in boiling water and season with salt and pepper. TO SERVE Divide the noodles between 2 soup plates. Cut each artichoke into 5 pieces and place them around the noodles. Whisk the coconut broth until frothy, then pour it on the noodles. Place the zucchini mash on the top of the noodles and drizzle a little rosemary oil around the dish. Garnish with truffle slices and serve immediately.

WINE 2002 St Clair Estate, Sauvignon Blanc, Marlborough, New Zealand

PAPILLOTE OF ASIAN VEGETABLES, WHOLE WHEAT RAVIOLI & COURT-BOUILLON

Serves 2

WHOLE WHEAT RAVIOLI
20 g / ¾ oz shallots, peeled and chopped
Olive oil for frying
80 g / 2⅞ oz shiitake mushrooms, chopped
80 g / 2⅞ oz oyster mushrooms, chopped
80 g / 2⅞ oz button mushrooms, chopped
80 g / 2⅞ oz roasted pine nuts
100 g / 3½ oz ricotta
10 sheets pasta (see Basics)
COURT-BOUILLON
500 ml / 17 fl oz / 2⅛ cups vegetable stock (see Basics)
80 g / 2⅞ oz celery, chopped
80 g / 2⅞ oz carrot, chopped
80 g / 2⅞ oz leek, chopped
80 g / 2⅞ oz onion, peeled and chopped
80 g / 2⅞ oz celeriac, peeled and chopped
1 oz chilli, sliced
50 g / 1⅜ oz lemon grass, chopped
50 g / 1⅜ oz galangal, sliced
3 tbsp black peppercorns
ASIAN VEGETABLES
80 g / 2⅞ oz whole zucchini
80 g / 2⅞ oz whole eggplant
40 g / 1¾ oz whole shiitake mushrooms
40 g / 1¾ oz spring onions
2 red chillies
1 yellow capsicum
1 green capsicum
1 red capsicum
80 g / 2⅞ oz whole cucumber
80 g / 2⅞ oz celery stalks
80 g / 2⅞ oz whole carrot
3 tbsp extra virgin olive oil
1 sprig coriander, chopped, for garnishing
1 bunch spring onions, chopped, for garnishing

Days at Koh Samui can be spent facing the coast in the cool shade of an umbrella. OPPOSITE: Papillote of Asian vegetables, whole wheat ravioli and court-bouillon.

WHOLE WHEAT RAVIOLI Sauté the shallots in some olive oil and add the mushrooms. Sauté until the mushrooms are cooked and remove them from the heat. Mix in the pine nuts and ricotta and shape the mixture into small, marble-sized balls. Place them on half a pasta sheet, maintaining 10 cm / 4 inches between fillings. Brush with water around each filling and cover with the other half of the pasta sheet. Press around each filling to seal each ravioli. Cut into squares or circles with a pastry cutter or knife. Place the ravioli on a tray dusted with a little flour, cover with a damp cloth and place the tray in the refrigerator until ready for use. COURT-BOUILLON Bring the vegetable stock to a boil. Add all the vegetables, herbs and peppercorns. Boil for at least 20 minutes for a tasty and slightly spicy broth. Meanwhile, blanch the ravioli in boiling water. They should be cooked short of al dente as they will finish cooking in the court-bouillon. ASIAN VEGETABLES Marinate all the whole vegetables in olive oil and grill. Once slightly blackened, slice into thin strips. Season with salt and pepper and set aside. ASSEMBLY Preheat oven to 250°C / 480°F. To prepare the papillote, place a sheet of greaseproof paper on a pan and place half of the vegetable strips and ravioli on it. Toss gently, taking care not to break the ravioli. Bring the corners and sides of the paper together and seal well, leaving just a tiny hole at the top for hot air to escape. Repeat with remaining vegetables and ravioli. Bake for about 5 to 8 minutes until piping hot. TO SERVE Heat the court-bouillon. Bring the hot pan to the table. Pour a little hot bouillon through the hole of the papillote in the pan. It should sizzle. Pour enough court-bouillon to wet the ravioli. Unwrap the papillote to release the aroma, then transfer the ravioli into soup plates. Ladle some hot court-bouillon over the ravioli and sprinkle chopped coriander and spring onion over to serve.

WINE 2002 Porta Italica, Pinot Grigio, Basilicata, Italy

PHUKET HAS BEEN called many things, among them Jewel of the Andaman and Pearl of the South. Located seven degrees north of the equator, it lies in the Andaman Sea, just off the west coast of southern Thailand. Phuket measures 539 square kilometres (approximately 208 square miles), and while it's renowned for its beaches, 80 percent of the terrain is mountainous. But it's the beaches and warm tropical weather that have made Phuket one of the world's most popular destinations, with over 4 million visitors in some years.

Tourism, however, brings with it changes. And while Phuket retains its position as the Jewel of the Andaman, it was not long ago that the jewel was lacking just a little lustre. Although many exclusive strips such as Surin Beach remained popular, neon lights and some more earthy aspects of nightlife made inroads into other areas, accompanied by an overabundance of shops stocking everything from cheap jewellery to imitation leather goods. Fortunately, the past few years have seen a renaissance of sorts, which is thanks mostly to the opening of a number of luxurious and exclusive resorts. Today, service and spa have become the current watchwords in the local hospitality trade, as each new resort tries its best to outdo its competitors.

The Evason Phuket Resort, situated on Rawai Beach which lies on the island's southeastern shore, has set itself apart from the rest. Set in the midst of approximately 26 hectares (64 acres) of landscaped tropical gardens, this resort and spa, formerly the Phuket Island Resort, has been recreated and redesigned by the Shivdasanis and their team to capture the essence of the Thai island holiday, while offering a new, refreshing concept in resort design.

Rawai Beach is a 45-minute drive from the airport. It's a quiet, peaceful stretch of beach just minutes from Promthep Cape, famed for its amazing sunset views. The Cape, once a beautiful and relaxed spot, has become overly popular with tourists. From the safe confines of the Evason, however, you can enjoy many magnificent sunsets without jostling for viewing space with throngs of sight-seers.

The entrance to the resort is reached by going up a hillock and through a coconut grove. The view from the hotel is stunning, and a central lotus pond looks out onto the Andaman Sea and over Laem Ka Beach, a smaller private beach at the end of Rawai. Check-ins are conducted in one of four open Thai salas (pavilions) set around the mirror-like pond.

From the main building, you're whisked away by buggy to one of the 260 rooms, suites and pool villas laid out across this lush property. While all Evason rooms face the sea, the seven pool villas here are the stars of the resort. The villas are closer to the beach than all other accommodations, with unparalleled views of the Andaman Sea, and a personal butler is in attendance at each villa. The overwhelming popularity of these villas prompted the resort to do a total makeover of all its superior rooms to create 21 pool duplex suites.

The design of Evason Phuket's pool villas certainly does not stint on space.
OPPOSITE: A tunnelled walkway brings guests from within the hotel to its lush gardens in dramatic style.

Even while you're enjoying these exclusive accommodations, do take some time to check into the Six Senses Spa. The spa treatment rooms include open-air salas set on a large lotus pond, accessible via small wooden walkways. As expected, the holistic treatments here are excellent, with an extensive range of therapies that will take you to heaven and back in one 80-minute session.

Evason Phuket also has four restaurants. Into the View, situated high above the sea, is the main restaurant and offers an international menu, as well as buffets on selected nights. Located on the water's edge, Into the Beach is set right along the beach, where a buffet lunch and dinner are served daily. You can sample sumptuous central Thai cuisine while enjoying the cool evening sea breeze at Into Thai.

More adventurous gourmands can make their way to Into Fushion. Open only at night, this beautifully designed space serves excellent food that combines Thai flavours and organically grown and raised local produce with Western culinary techniques and presentation.

If, however, you're looking for a singular experience, book the resort's Honeymoon Suite and arrange for a private candlelit dinner under the stars on Bon Island. Bon Island is a short 15-minute boat ride from the hotel, and is exclusively for the use of its guests, with its powdery white sands and fantastic snorkelling opportunities. Ten day salas sit on Bon Island, perfect for chilling out and doing nothing in. By night, however, the island is entirely different. Magical, mysterious and romantic, this tiny island was made for couples, which is why the Shivdasanis have built only one villa here. The Honeymoon Suite sits on stilts in the jungle, lying 30 metres (98 feet) above the beach and offering unimpeded views of the Andaman Sea. Booking the Suite also means booking Bon Island exclusively for you and your loved one.

Evason Phuket is one reason that the Jewel of the Andaman is sparkling again. As for the others, you'll have to make the trip to find out.

SMOKED SALMON & CAVIAR ON BLINIS *Serves 8*

BLINIS
1 egg yolk, beaten
½ tsp sugar
60 ml / 2 fl oz / ¼ cup lukewarm water
50 g / 1¾ oz / ⅓ cup buckwheat flour or half-and-half with plain flour
A pinch of dried yeast
Salt to taste
60 ml / 2 fl oz / ¼ cup lukewarm milk
1 tbsp butter for frying
TOPPINGS & ACCOMPANIMENTS
50 g / 1¾ oz smoked salmon, finely sliced
200 ml / 6¾ ml / ⅞ cup sour cream
50 g / 1¾ oz Sevruga caviar
50 g / 1¾ oz salmon roe
20 g / ¾ oz fresh herbs (chives and dill), chopped

BLINIS Whisk the egg yolk, sugar and water in a mixing bowl. Mix the flour, yeast and salt in a separate bowl and make a well in the centre. Pour the egg mixture into the well and mix thoroughly. Cover with a damp cloth and let rise at room temperature for about 2 hours until it has doubled in volume. Whisk in the milk until thick and creamy. Cover again and leave for 1 hour or until small bubbles appear on the surface. Heat a frying pan and brush with butter. Drop about 1 tsp of batter on the pan to make a pancake about 2.5 cm / 1 inch in diameter. Cook until the surface bubbles, about 2 to 3 minutes, then flip it over with a palette knife and cook the second side for about 2 minutes. Place the prepared blinis on a plate in a warm oven while preparing the rest. Do not stack them up. (Blinis can be stored in an airtight container for up to 3 days. To serve, reheat them for 5 minutes in a preheated oven at 200°C / 400°F.) TO SERVE Top the warm blinis with smoked salmon. Serve on a platter accompanied by cream, caviar, salmon roe and fresh herbs.

WINE NV Veuve Cliquot Ponsardin Brut Champagne, Rheims, France

SMOKED SALMON & OMELETTE ROLL ON CUCUMBER RINGS *Serves 8*

OMELETTE
4 eggs, beaten
Salt and pepper to taste
Butter or olive oil for frying
FILLING
2 sheets nori
200 g / 7 oz smoked salmon
16 stalks spring onions, roots removed
40 g / 1⅜ oz carrot, peeled and cut into thin strips
2 whole cucumbers, sliced into 2.5 cm / 1 inch sections, seeds removed
Few drops of sesame oil for garnishing

OMELETTE Season the beaten eggs with salt and pepper. Pour a thin layer of this mixture into a heated frying pan brushed with oil or butter. Cook until the omelette has just set, then slide it out onto a large plate and let cool. Repeat with the remaining egg. FILLING Place the seaweed on the omelettes, followed by layers of salmon, spring onions and carrot, and roll up. The diameter of the omelette roll must be a little smaller than the cucumber rounds. Tie the roll up in 4 places using 4 spring onion leaves as ribbons. Slice into 4 equal portions. Repeat with the other omelette. TO SERVE Arrange the cucumber slices on a serving tray. Top each one with a roll of omelette. Dress each with a drop of sesame oil.

WINE 2000 Viñedos y Crianzas del Alto Aragón, Enate Unoaked Chardonnay 234, Somontano, Spain

THAI CRAB CAKES WITH CHILLI SAUCE *Serves 8*

THAI CRAB CAKES
1 red chilli, seeds removed
1 bunch spring onions, chopped
1 clove garlic, peeled and crushed
1 stalk coriander, chopped
Thumb-sized piece of ginger or galangal, peeled and chopped
1 kaffir lime leaf, finely sliced, or zest of 1 lime
1 tsp fish sauce
60 g / 2⅛ oz cod fish fillet, chopped
60 g / 2⅛ oz / ⅓ cup crabmeat
1 long bean, finely sliced
10 g / ⅜ oz vermicelli, soaked in hot water for 5 minutes
1 tbsp beaten egg
Oil for frying
CHILLI SAUCE
2 tbsp white rice vinegar
1 red chilli, finely sliced
1 tsp fish sauce
1 spring onion, finely sliced
½ tsp brown sugar
1 small onion, peeled and finely diced for garnishing
1 red chilli, seeds removed and finely diced for garnishing
1 bunch spring onions, chopped for garnishing

THAI CRAB CAKES Process the chilli, spring onions, garlic, coriander, ginger or galangal, kaffir lime leaf or lime zest and fish sauce in a blender until you get a smooth paste. Add the fish and process until well blended. Transfer the mixture to a bowl and add the crabmeat and bean. Mix well. Drain the vermicelli and snip into short pieces about 3 cm / 1.2 inches long. Add them to the fish mixture and stir in the beaten egg thoroughly. Make small cakes with 1 to 2 tbsp of the mixture. Wet your hands with water before shaping the paste into patties. (You may sprinkle the patties with rice flour before frying if you want them to be extra crisp.) Pan-fry or deep-fry the crab cakes in a hot pan or wok until they begin to brown. Keep the fried crab cakes warm in the oven while preparing the remaining mixture. CHILLI SAUCE Mix the sauce ingredients together in a small bowl. TO SERVE Arrange crab cakes on a serving plate. Garnish with chopped onions, chilli and a curl of spring onion and serve with chilli sauce on the side.

WINE 2000 Domaine Zind Humbrecht Clos Hauserer Riesling, Alsace, France

The décor at Into Fushion combines minimalism with warmth and intimacy. OPPOSITE: Smoked salmon and caviar on blinis; Smoked salmon and omelette roll on cucumber rings; Thai crab cakes with chilli sauce.

Beef fillet and shiitake mushrooms in miso sauce with white bean and coriander mash.
OPPOSITE: Nage of white miso with mussels, scallops, red snapper and river prawns.

BEEF FILLET & SHIITAKE MUSHROOMS IN MISO SAUCE WITH WHITE BEAN & CORIANDER MASH Serves 2

WHITE BEAN & CORIANDER MASH
300 g / 10½ oz potatoes, unpeeled
50 to 100 ml / 1¾ to 3⅜ fl oz / ¼ to ⅜ cup hot skimmed milk
100 g / 3½ oz cooked white beans
2 stalks fresh coriander, finely sliced
Salt and pepper to taste
BEEF FILLET & SHIITAKE MUSHROOMS
2 (each about 200 g / 7 oz) beef fillets
1 tsp olive oil
1 onion, peeled and diced
250 g / 8⅞ oz shiitake mushrooms
1 heaped tbsp dark red miso paste
1 tbsp brown sugar
120 ml / 4 fl oz / ½ cup hot water
2 tbsp shredded red capsicum for garnishing

WHITE BEAN & CORIANDER MASH
Cook the potatoes in boiling salted water for 30 minutes or until tender. Drain and return the potatoes to the pot. Shake the pot over low heat for 1 minute until the excess water evaporates. Mash the potatoes with a ricer. With a wooden spoon, blend in the hot skimmed milk. Add the white beans and coriander. Season with salt and pepper. Keep warm and covered over a bain marie or pot of hot water. BEEF FILLET & SHIITAKE MUSHROOMS In a very hot pan, sear the beef with olive oil for a few minutes. Add the onions and continue to cook over medium heat until the beef is almost cooked to desired doneness. Sprinkle a little water over while cooking. Add the shiitake mushrooms and cook for another minute while continuing to sprinkle water occasionally to keep the food moist. Combine the miso, sugar and water in a bowl, mix well and add to the beef. Cook for another minute, adding more water if it is too salty. TO SERVE Spoon dollops of mashed potatoes onto serving dishes, top with beef, shiitake mushrooms and sauce. Garnish with capsicum shreds.

WINE 2001 Plantagenet Shiraz, Mount Barker, Western Australia

NAGE OF WHITE MISO WITH MUSSELS, SCALLOPS, RED SNAPPER & RIVER PRAWNS

Serves 2

NAGE OF WHITE MISO
200 ml / 6¾ fl oz / ⅞ cup fish stock (see Basics)
5 tsp shiro miso paste
2 tsp hon dashi granules
1 stalk lemon grass, sliced
1 tbsp Japanese rice wine vinegar
5 tsp whipping cream
30 g / 1 oz butter
Salt and pepper to taste
SEAFOOD
4 mussels
2 river prawns
40 g / 1⅜ oz red snapper fillet, sliced
2 large scallops
VEGETABLES
4 spears Thai asparagus, blanched
4 cherry tomatoes, halved
A few sticks of fried buckwheat noodles for garnishing
2 strips nori for tying fried buckwheat noodles

NAGE OF WHITE MISO Place the fish stock, miso paste, dashi granules and lemon grass in a saucepan and simmer for 10 minutes. Strain the stock. Add the vinegar, cream and butter to the liquid and cook for another 5 minutes. Season with salt and pepper. SEAFOOD Poach the mussels, river prawns and snapper in the miso broth until just cooked and keep warm. Season the scallops and grill for 2 minutes on each side, or until just cooked. VEGETABLES Bring the miso broth to a boil and reheat the asparagus in it. Strain the broth again. TO SERVE Divide the asparagus between 2 soup plates. Add the tomatoes and poached seafood and ladle miso broth over. Garnish with fried buckwheat noodles fastened together with nori strip.

WINE 2000 Cairnbrae 'Old River' Riesling, Marlborough, New Zealand

GREEN TEA NOODLE SUSHI WITH CUCUMBER, AVOCADO & WASABI MAYONNAISE Serves 2

WASABI MAYONNAISE
2 tsp soy mayonnaise
A pinch of wasabi paste
GREEN TEA NOODLE SUSHI
120 g / 4¼ oz green tea noodles
Sesame oil to taste
A slice of pickled ginger, finely diced
2 sheets nori
½ Japanese cucumber, peeled, cut lengthwise into thin strips as long as nori sheets
¼ avocado, cut into strips
2 shiitake mushrooms, thinly sliced
Soy sauce for dipping
1 mound pickled ginger

WASABI MAYONNAISE Combine the wasabi mayonnaise ingredients and set aside. GREEN TEA NOODLE SUSHI Cook the noodles in boiling salted water until al dente. Drain and rinse under cold water. Drain again and toss with the sesame oil and ginger. Rest noodles at room temperature for 15 minutes. Place a sheet of nori on a bamboo sushi mat and place a layer of noodles over half of the sheet. Spread 1 tsp of wasabi mayonnaise over the noodles. Arrange slices of cucumber, avocado and mushroom on top of the noodles. Roll the sushi up firmly using the bamboo mat. Repeat with the remaining nori sheet. Cut each nori roll into 6 to 8 portions. TO SERVE Present sushi rolls with soy sauce, pickled ginger and other condiments of your choice.

WINE 2000 Revereto Gavi del Commune di Gavi, Michele Chiarlo, Piedmont, Italy

LIME & GREEN TEA TIRAMISU

Serves 2

LIME & GREEN TEA TIRAMISU
100 g / 3½ oz / ⅜ cup cream cheese
2 tbsp caster sugar
2 tbsp lime juice
Zest from 1 lime
⅓ packet of lime jelly crystals
A pinch of green tea powder
4 tsp hot water
1 egg white, beaten to soft peaks
Enough sponge finger biscuits to fill a small loaf tin
40 ml / 1⅜ fl oz / ¼ cup Midori liqueur
Icing sugar for dusting
A few sticks of fried buckwheat noodles for garnishing
2 strips nori for garnishing

LIME & GREEN TEA TIRAMISU Process the cheese, sugar, lime juice and zest in a blender until smooth. In a bowl, dissolve the jelly crystals and green tea powder in the hot water. Add this to the cheese mixture and blend well. Fold this mixture into the beaten egg white. Line a short loaf tin with 2 sheets of plastic wrap. Dip the sponge fingers briefly into the Midori and arrange them to cover the base of the tin. Pour enough of the cheese mixture to cover the biscuits. Keep layering biscuits and mixture until the tin is full or the mixture is used up. Finish with a layer of biscuits. Set overnight in the refrigerator. TO SERVE Place a slice of cake on a serving plate and dust with icing sugar then drizzle Midori liqueur around. Garnish with fried buckwheat noodles bound with a strip of nori.

WINE 1996 Vendange Tardive Hugel Riesling, Alsace, France

Lime and green tea tiramisu.
OPPOSITE: Green tea noodle sushi with cucumber, avocado and wasabi mayonnaise.

GRILLED PINEAPPLE WITH MANGO, GINGER & CHILLI SORBET Serves 2

MANGO, GINGER & CHILLI SORBET
1 whole mango, peeled and seed removed
1 tbsp finely grated ginger root
1 kaffir lime leaf, stem removed
½ red chilli, seeds removed
2 tbsp lime juice
1 tbsp clear honey
30 g / 1 oz / ⅛ cup finely grated palm sugar
GRILLED PINEAPPLE
½ pineapple, cut into wedges, cored and peeled
30 g / 1 oz / ⅛ cup finely grated palm sugar
2 red chilli curls for garnishing

MANGO, GINGER & CHILLI SORBET
Process all the ingredients, except the palm sugar, in a blender for 2 minutes, then add the palm sugar and blend for a further 20 seconds. Pour the mixture into an ice cream machine and follow the manufacturer's directions (about 30 to 45 minutes). Keep frozen until required. GRILLED PINEAPPLE Lay the pineapple wedges on a tray and sprinkle with the palm sugar. Cover with plastic wrap and leave for 1 hour to marinate. Preheat the grill on high or use a very hot charcoal grill. Grill the marinated pineapple on all sides until it begins to caramelise. Transfer to a plate and let cool. Reserve any roasting juices and pour over the pineapple. TO SERVE Place a wedge of grilled pineapple on a plate and top with a scoop of sorbet. Garnish with a red chilli curl.

WINE 2001 Domaine Jaffelin, St-Romain, Burgundy, France

Undulating drapes and well-placed lighting accentuate the airy, spacious feel of the suite.
OPPOSITE (CLOCKWISE FROM LEFT): Grilled pineapple with mango, ginger and chilli sorbet; Roasted rack of lamb and eggplant caviar with tamarind-port sauce; Baked snapper with green tea noodles and lime salsa.

ROASTED RACK OF LAMB & EGGPLANT CAVIAR WITH TAMARIND-PORT SAUCE Serves 2

ROASTED RACK OF LAMB
1 lamb rack of Frenched-8 ribs, trimmed
40 ml / 1⅜ fl oz / ¼ cup cranberry mustard
1 tsp coriander seeds, coarsely ground
1 tsp fennel seeds, coarsely ground
1 tsp cumin seeds, coarsely ground
½ tsp black peppercorns, freshly cracked
Salt to taste
SHALLOT-GARLIC CONFIT
60 g / 2⅛ oz shallots, peeled
40 ml / 1⅜ fl oz / ¼ cup cassis wine
50 ml / 1¾ fl oz / ¼ cup red wine
3 tbsp pine nuts, toasted
1 tbsp sultanas
Salt and pepper to taste
40 g / 1⅜ oz garlic cloves, unpeeled
50 ml / 1¾ oz / ¼ cup olive oil
A few sprigs of thyme
EGGPLANT CAVIAR
½ tsp chopped garlic
A pinch of chopped thyme
A pinch of chopped rosemary
40 ml / 1⅜ fl oz / ¼ cup olive oil
1½ tbsp finely diced red capsicum
1½ tbsp finely diced green capsicum
1½ tbsp finely diced yellow capsicum
1½ tbsp finely diced shiitake mushrooms
300 g / 10½ oz eggplant, roasted and peeled
Salt and pepper to taste
TAMARIND-PORT SAUCE
50 g / 1¾ oz tamarind pulp
25 g / ⅞ oz shallots, peeled and sliced
1 stalk lemon grass, sliced
Thumb-size piece of blue ginger, peeled and sliced
100 ml / 3⅜ fl oz / ⅜ cup red wine
100 ml / 3⅜ fl oz / ⅜ cup port wine
25 g / ⅞ oz butter
2 tbsp basil oil for garnishing
A few sprigs of deep-fried flat parsley for garnishing

ROASTED RACK OF LAMB Preheat oven to 170°C / 340°F. Brush the lamb with cranberry mustard and coat it with the ground spices. Pan-fry the lamb rack over medium heat until golden brown, then roast for 20 to 25 minutes or until desired doneness. Reserve the baking juices. SHALLOT AND GARLIC CONFIT Cook the shallots with cassis and red wine over low heat until they caramelise. Add pine nuts and sultanas. Season with salt and pepper. Fry the garlic cloves with a little olive oil and thyme at high heat to brown the skin. Add the rest of the olive oil quickly to bring down the temperature. Finish cooking the garlic in the oven for 20 to 30 minutes at 150°C / 300°F until soft. Drain and keep warm. EGGPLANT CAVIAR Sweat the garlic and herbs in olive oil until fragrant. Mix in the capsicums and mushrooms. Mix with the eggplant flesh. Season with salt and pepper. TAMARIND-PORT SAUCE Sauté the tamarind pulp, shallots, lemon grass and blue ginger for 2 minutes, then deglaze with red wine and port. Reduce the wine by a third and add 150 ml / 5 fl oz / ⅝ cup of the reserved lamb's baking juices. Continue to reduce the sauce to desired consistency. Strain through a fine-mesh sieve and whisk in butter. TO SERVE Place 2 tbsps of eggplant caviar on each plate. Drizzle some basil oil over them and garnish with fried parsley. Slice the lamb rack into individual cutlets and arrange them in the centre of the plate. Pour some tamarind-port sauce over and garnish with shallot and garlic confit.

WINE 1998 Weingut Prieler Cabernet Sauvignon, Ungerbergen, Austria

BAKED SNAPPER WITH GREEN TEA NOODLES & LIME SALSA Serves 2

LIME SALSA
2 tbsp finely chopped red capsicum
2 tbsp finely chopped yellow capsicum
2 tbsp chopped chives
2 tbsp chopped red onion
1 clove garlic, peeled and crushed
Juice from 2 limes
1 tsp olive oil
½ tsp honey
Sea salt to taste
BAKED SNAPPER
2 (each about 180 g / 6⅜ oz) snapper fillets
4 tbsp mirin
2 tbsp soy sauce
Juice from 1 lime
1 tsp olive oil
GREEN TEA NOODLES
200 g / 7 oz green tea noodles
2 tbsp chopped coriander
½ tsp sesame oil
Sea salt to taste

LIME SALSA Combine all ingredients in a bowl and set aside. BAKED SNAPPER Marinate the snapper in mirin, soy sauce and lime juice for 30 minutes. Preheat oven to 200°C / 400°F. Heat olive oil in a pan and sear the skin side of the fish for 1 to 2 minutes until golden. Turn it over and place on an oven tray. Finish cooking in the oven for 5 to 10 minutes. GREEN TEA NOODLES Cook noodles in boiling salted water until al dente. Drain and toss with coriander, sesame oil and sea salt. TO SERVE Divide the noodles between 2 plates and set the baked snapper fillets on the side. Spoon some salsa around and over.

WINE 2002 Cranswick Estate Unoaked Botrytis Semillon, Riverina, Australia

KAFFIR LIME-BASIL PARFAIT WITH PINEAPPLE COMPOTE
Serves 2

KAFFIR LIME-BASIL PARFAIT
4 tsp water
3 basil leaves
1 egg yolk
6 tsp granulated sugar
4 tsp kaffir lime juice
Zest from 1 kaffir lime
5½ tbsp whipping cream
PINEAPPLE COMPOTE
5 tbsp water
1 tbsp sugar
50 g / 1¾ oz pineapple, peeled and cut into strips
1 basil leaf, cut into thin strips
STRAWBERRY JUS
2 tbsp sugar
160 g / 5⅝ oz frozen strawberries
SAGO
1 tbsp sago pearls, soaked in water for 30 minutes
100 ml / 3⅜ fl oz / ⅜ cup water
ORANGE TUILE
1 tsp flour
2 tsp granulated sugar
2 tsp icing sugar
1 tbsp orange juice
2 tsp melted butter
1 strawberry, cut into wedges for garnishing
4 chocolate sticks for garnishing
4 sprigs deep-fried basil for garnishing

KAFFIR LIME-BASIL PARFAIT Boil the water and add basil leaves. Remove from heat and infuse for 10 minutes. Process in a blender until smooth. Strain into a heat-proof bowl. Add egg yolk, 4 tsp of sugar and lime juice and whisk in a bain marie until pale and fluffy. Transfer to another bowl and whisk until cool. Add the zest. Whip the cream with the remaining sugar. Fold this into the basil mixture. Pipe into ring moulds, 5 cm / 2 inches wide and as tall. Freeze. PINEAPPLE COMPOTE Boil water and sugar in a small pan. Add pineapple and basil, and simmer until the syrup is reduced by half. Mash pineapple with a·wooden spoon. Remove from heat before it dries out. STRAWBERRY JUS Combine sugar and strawberries in a heat-proof bowl. Place in a pan of simmering water for 1 hour until the strawberries soften. Strain and chill the liquid in an ice bath. SAGO Drain the sago and cook in boiling water until transparent. Drain and rinse the sago under running water. Let cool. ORANGE TUILE Combine the flour, sugar and icing sugar. Stir in orange juice and butter. Let it rest for 2 hours. Spread a thin layer on a non-stick baking sheet. Bake at 180°C / 350°F until golden. TO SERVE Serve parfaît with sago, strawberry jus and pineapple compôte. Garnish with tuile, strawberries, chocolate sticks and basil.

WINE 1994 Königschaffhausen Hasenberg Ruländer Beerenauslese, Baden, Germany

ROASTED BLACK COD & GAZPACHO HASH WITH RED CURRY SABAYON Serves 2

RED CURRY SABAYON
2 egg yolks
2 tsp white wine
½ tsp red curry paste
2 tsp olive oil
Juice from ½ lemon
Sugar, salt and pepper to taste
GAZPACHO HASH
2 medium potatoes, peeled
1 tomato, peeled, seeds and pulp removed, diced
½ cucumber, peeled, seeds removed and diced
1 tbsp finely chopped parsley
1 clove garlic, peeled and finely chopped
1 small red onion, peeled and finely chopped
Salt and pepper to taste
ROASTED BLACK COD
350 g / 12⅜ oz black cod fillet, cut into 2 portions
Oil for roasting
Salt and pepper to taste
2 long slices of sautéed eggplant for garnishing
A few sprigs of fried parsley leaves for garnishing

RED CURRY SABAYON Whisk the egg yolks with the wine in a stainless steel mixing bowl. Set the bowl in a bain marie and cook, stirring constantly for about 8 minutes or until the mixture is thick and frothy. Turn the heat off, but leave the bowl in the bain marie to keep warm. Stir in the curry paste, olive oil, lemon juice and sugar. Season with salt and pepper. Keep warm, stirring occasionally. GAZPACHO HASH Cook the potatoes in boiling salted water until soft. Drain, then return to the pan and mash roughly. Mix in the remaining hash ingredients. Season with salt and pepper and keep warm. ROASTED BLACK COD Preheat the oven to 180°C / 350°F. Brush the fish with oil and season with salt and pepper. Place the fish on a baking tray and cook in the oven for 10 to 15 minutes or until almost cooked. Transfer to a flameproof platter. Preheat the grill. Liberally pour most of the sabayon over the fish and grill until golden. Alternatively, brown the fish using a blowtorch. TO SERVE Place a serving of hash in the centre of each plate. Place a portion of fish on the hash. Top with a roll of eggplant and sprinkle with fried parsley leaves. Drizzle some sabayon around and serve the remaining sabayon on the side.

WINE 1998 Mount Pleasant Elizabeth Semillon, Hunter Valley, Australia

OPPOSITE (CLOCKWISE FROM TOP LEFT): Kaffir lime-basil parfaît with pineapple compôte; Salmon trout confit and spicy eggplant with calamansi lime and butter sauce; Roasted black cod and gazpacho hash with red curry sabayon.

SALMON TROUT CONFIT & SPICY EGGPLANT WITH CALAMANSI LIME & BUTTER SAUCE Serves 2

SALMON TROUT CONFIT
2 (each about 120 g / 4¼ oz) Tasmanian salmon trout fillets
250 ml / 8½ fl oz / 1 cup olive oil
1 tbsp rock salt
½ tsp pink peppercorns
1 dried chilli
1 tbsp grated coriander root
½ tsp lime zest
SPICY EGGPLANT
50 g / 1¾ oz red onion, peeled and diced
½ tsp chopped garlic
½ tsp minced young ginger
150 g / 5¼ oz eggplant, sliced
1 tbsp Chinese hua tiao wine or sherry
40 ml / 1⅜ fl oz / ¼ cup chilli broad bean paste
1 tbsp oyster sauce
2 tsp Chinese black vinegar
Salt, pepper and sugar to taste
CALAMANSI LIME & BUTTER SAUCE
100 ml / 3⅜ fl oz / ⅜ cup white wine
100 ml / 3⅜ fl oz / ⅜ cup white wine vinegar
3 black peppercorns, crushed
100 g / 3⅜ oz butter
1 tbsp calamansi juice
A pinch of grated calamansi zest
Salt and pepper to taste
40 g / 1⅜ oz string beans, sliced and blanched
40 g / 1⅜ oz red capsicum, thinly sliced
A few sprigs of fried coriander leaves
2 sticks cinnamon for garnishing
2 star anise pods for garnishing
A pinch of rock salt

SALMON TROUT CONFIT Soak the fish with the olive oil, rock salt, pink peppercorns, dried chilli, coriander root and lime zest in an oven-proof dish. Keep refrigerated for at least 1 hour before use. Keep the fish at room temperature for 30 minutes before use. Preheat oven to 80°C / 180°F. Bake the fish with the marinade for 10 to 15 minutes or until just cooked. Drain off excess oil. SPICY EGGPLANT Sauté the onions, garlic and ginger in a wok over medium heat until lightly brown. Add the eggplant and continue to sauté. Deglaze with rice wine or sherry and add the remaining ingredients. Cook until eggplant is soft. Season with salt, pepper and sugar. CALAMANSI LIME & BUTTER SAUCE Combine the wine, vinegar and peppercorns in a pan and simmer until liquid is reduced by half. Whisk in the cold butter. Add the calamansi juice and zest. Season. TO SERVE Heap 1 tbsp of spicy eggplant on a plate and top with the salmon trout. Drizzle sauce and top with string beans, capsicum, herbs and salt.

WINE 2000 Santa Cecilia Sauvignon Blanc-Colombard, Guadalupe, Mexico

KAI HIMMAPAN (STIR-FRIED CHICKEN & CASHEWS) Serves 4

MARINATED CHICKEN
4 cloves garlic, peeled and crushed
2 tsp light soy sauce
1 tsp ground white pepper
600 g / 1 lb 5⅛ oz skinless chicken breast, sliced
KAI HIMMAPAN
6 tbsp cashew nuts
Vegetable oil for frying
80 g / 2⅞ oz Spanish onion, peeled and sliced
240 g / 8½ oz / 1½ cups red, green and yellow capsicums, sliced
1 large carrot, cut into matchstick-sized strips
8 baby corns, quartered
16 button mushrooms, quartered
4 bunches spring onions, sliced
120 g / 4¼ oz pineapple, cut into small pieces
8 tbsp chicken stock (see Basics)
6 tbsp oyster sauce
6 tbsp Blue Elephant special sauce or Maggi seasoning
4 cinnamon sticks for garnishing
4 lime leaves for garnishing
4 slices lime for garnishing

MARINATED CHICKEN Mix the garlic with the soy sauce and pepper. Marinate the chicken with this for 15 minutes. KAI HIMMAPAN Fry the cashew nuts briefly in a small amount of oil until slightly browned and set aside. Stir-fry all the vegetables and set aside. Heat 3 tbsp of oil in a wok until very hot. Add the marinated chicken and stir-fry for 30 seconds. Add the stock and sauce and cook for 1 minute or until the chicken is cooked through. Mix in the cashew nuts. TO SERVE Place the vegetables in a serving dish and top with chicken and cashew nuts. Garnish with the cinnamon sticks, lime leaves and slices.

WINE 2002 Shala One Red Blend Dongjaroen, Pichit, Thailand

Organic sculptures flank the tunnel that leads to the hotel lobby.
OPPOSITE (CLOCKWISE FROM TOP): Steamed rice; Tom yum koong (Sour and spicy prawn soup); Kruay chu'am (Caramelised bananas); Kai himmapan (Stir-fried chicken and cashews); Tow-hu peaw wan (Sweet and sour tofu); Tod man pla (Thai fish cakes).

KRUAY CHU'AM (CARAMELISED BANANAS) Serves 4

KRUAY CHU'AM
225 g / 8⅛ oz / 1⅛ cups granulated sugar
225 ml / 7½ fl oz / 1 cup water
4 large bananas, peeled and cut into 5-cm / 2-inch pieces
Salt to taste
4 cinnamon sticks for garnishing
4 star anise pods for garnishing

KRUAY CHU'AM Mix the sugar and water in a saucepan and simmer until all the sugar has dissolved. Bring to a boil. Add the bananas and lower the heat. Simmer until the syrup forms threads when a wooden spoon is dipped in and lifted from it. Skim off any froth that floats to the surface. Season with a little salt. TO SERVE Transfer to serving bowls and garnish with the cinnamon sticks and star anise pods.

WINE NV Chandon Estate Cava Eclipse, Spain

TOD MAN PLA (THAI FISH CAKES) Serves 4

TOD MAN PLA
100 g / 3½ oz cod fillet, chopped
100 g / 3½ oz squid, chopped
1 tbsp red curry paste
½ tbsp fish sauce
1 tsp sugar
1 kaffir lime leaf, finely chopped
30 g / 1 oz French beans, sliced thinly
1 tbsp beaten egg
Vegetable oil for deep-frying
¼ tsp crushed roasted peanuts for garnishing
Wedge of lime or lemon for garnishing
A few red chilli strips for garnishing

TOD MAN PLA Blend the fish and squid into a smooth paste. Mix in the curry paste, fish sauce, sugar, lime leaf and beans. Fold in the egg. Shape the mixture into 4 discs, then deep-fry until golden. TO SERVE Sprinkle with peanuts and garnish with the citrus wedge and chilli strips.

WINE 2002 Château de Loei Chenin Blanc, Loei, Thailand

TOM YUM KOONG (SOUR & SPICY PRAWN SOUP) Serves 4

TOM YUM KOONG
2 small green chillies
1 bunch coriander root and stems
300 ml / 10⅛ fl oz / 1¼ cups chicken stock (see Basics)
6 slivers galangal
1 stalk lemon grass, finely chopped
2 kaffir lime leaves
4 small button mushrooms, quartered
8 king prawns, shelled with tails intact and deveined
1 tbsp fish sauce
2 tsp lemon juice
1 tsp nam prik phao (sweet chilli paste)
Fresh coriander leaves for garnishing

TOM YUM KOONG In a mortar, crush the green chillies with the coriander root and stems. Bring the stock to a boil in a pan. Add the galangal, lemon grass, kaffir lime leaves and mushrooms and bring to a boil again. Add the prawns, fish sauce, crushed chillies and coriander roots and stems, lemon juice and nam prik phao and simmer for 1 minute. TO SERVE Serve the hot soup in 2 bowls and garnish with coriander leaves.

WINE 2001 Pine Ridge Chenin Blanc-Viognier, California, USA

TOW-HU PEAW WAN (SWEET & SOUR TOFU) Serves 4

TOW-HU PEAW WAN
320 g / 11¼ oz beancurd, cubed
Vegetable oil for deep-frying
4 tbsp vegetable oil
2 cucumber slices
2 tomato slices
120 g / 4¼ oz / 1 cup mixed capsicums, sliced
15 button mushrooms, quartered
20 baby corns, quartered
4 bunches spring onions, sliced
2 onions, peeled and sliced
1 small piece root ginger, peeled and cut into matchstick-sized strips
500 ml / 17 fl oz / 2⅛ cups instant sweet and sour sauce
Coriander leaves for garnishing

TOW-HU PEAW WAN Deep-fry the beancurd in oil until golden. Remove and set on kitchen paper to draw out excess oil. Stir-fry all the vegetables and ginger in a very hot pan for 30 seconds. Add the sweet and sour sauce, and bring to a boil. Transfer to a serving dish. TO SERVE Add the tofu to the vegetables and garnish with coriander leaves.

WINE 1999 Springfield Estate Méthode Ancienne Chardonnay, Robertson, South Africa

LEMON GRASS LASAGNA WITH ORGANIC VEGETABLES & COCONUT BECHAMEL SAUCE Serves 2

LEMON GRASS LASAGNA
500 g / 1 lb 1⅝ oz / 4 cups bread flour
5 eggs
½ tbsp olive oil
80 g / 2⅞ oz lemon grass, finely chopped
Salt to taste

COCONUT BECHAMEL SAUCE
150 g / 5⅓ oz / 1⅛ cups plain flour
120 g / 4¼ oz / ½ cup melted butter
100 ml / 3⅜ fl oz / ⅜ cup coconut milk
1 stalk lemon grass, crushed
Salt and pepper to taste

ORGANIC VEGETABLES
2 organic red capsicums, grilled and sliced
1 organic zucchini, thinly sliced
1 organic carrot, thinly sliced
100 ml / 3⅜ fl oz / ⅜ cup olive oil
2 cloves garlic, peeled and crushed
100 g / 3½ oz organic bok choy
250 g / 8⅞ oz organic tomatoes, peeled, seeds
and pulp removed, and chopped
Parmesan shavings for garnishing
4 organic cherry tomatoes, halved for garnishing
½ stalk lemon grass, thinly sliced for garnishing

LEMON GRASS LASAGNA Mix the flour and eggs. Add olive oil, lemon grass and salt. Knead and flatten to a 0.2-cm- / 0.1-inch-thick layer. Cut into 12 discs measuring 8 cm / 3 inches in diameter. Blanch lasagna sheets in boiling salted water. COCONUT BECHAMEL SAUCE Mix flour with melted butter over low heat and whisk until it thickens. Slowly add the coconut milk, followed by the lemon grass. Mix well and season with salt and pepper. ORGANIC VEGETABLES Preheat grill. Marinate the capsicums, zucchini and carrot in olive oil and garlic. Grill the vegetables until they soften. TO SERVE Blanch bok choy in boiling salted water. Place a layer of lasagna on a plate. Spread the chopped tomato and coconut béchamel sauce on it. Arrange a layer of grilled organic vegetables on this. Top with another sheet of lasagna. Repeat layers twice more. On the topmost layer of lasagna, finish with a topping of bok choy and Parmesan shavings. Garnish with cherry tomatoes and a sprinkling of sliced lemon grass.

WINE 2002 Vignerons de St Tropez, Côtes de Provence, France

The rugged elegance of a driftwood sculpture set in a wall niche is in keeping with the natural décor elements which dominate the resort.
OPPOSITE: Lemon grass lasagna with organic vegetables and coconut béchamel sauce.

Comfortable wooden loungers let
guests laze by the shimmering waters
of the pool.
OPPOSITE: Silken tofu and shiitake
mushrooms with green vegetables.

SILKEN TOFU & SHIITAKE MUSHROOMS WITH GREEN VEGETABLES Serves 2

SILKEN TOFU & SHIITAKE MUSHROOMS
WITH GREEN VEGETABLES
1 clove garlic, peeled and crushed
½ tsp olive oil
60 ml / 2 fl oz / ¼ cup vegetable or chicken stock
(see Basics)
120 g / 4¼ oz small shiitake mushrooms
1 bunch spinach leaves, washed
1 witlof, separated into leaves
1 tbsp vegetarian oyster sauce
160 g / 5⅝ oz silken tofu
A handful of snow pea sprouts for garnishing
A handful of bean sprouts for garnishing
A few slices of pickled ginger for garnishing
2 sprigs of parsley for garnishing

SILKEN TOFU & SHIITAKE MUSHROOMS
WITH GREEN VEGETABLES Sauté the garlic
in olive oil with a little vegetable or chicken stock
until it is soft. Add the mushrooms and cook for 1
minute. Add the spinach and witlof leaves and
cook until just wilted, adding a little stock if
necessary. Add the oyster sauce and toss well. Cut
the tofu into 4 pieces and add them to the greens.
TO SERVE Garnish with sprouts, pickled ginger
and parsley.

WINE 2000 Enate Rosado Cabernet Sauvignon,
Somontano, Spain

IT WOULD BE pretty fair to say that many of us would love to live like kings. While this still remains, for most, merely an idle dream, more and more things are possible these days. Rock stars, movie stars and other celebrities have shown us that much of the high life is now accessible to anyone who can afford it.

Nowhere is that more true than at Hua Hin, where the Thai Royal Family have been taking their holidays for over eight decades. This beautiful stretch of land, overlooking the Gulf of Thailand and approximately 200 kilometres

(124 miles) southwest of Bangkok, is Thailand's oldest beach resort area. It was first made popular in the early 1920s, thanks in part to the development of the Southern Railroad, which linked the country overland from the capital all the way through to Malaysia.

It was no less than a prince who put Hua Hin on the map. In 1923, Prince Purachatra, Director General of the State Railways, built and opened the Railway Hotel, a stunning Victorian-style building complete with manicured gardens and the country's first golf course. Soon enough, all of Bangkok's elite were vacationing at Hua Hin. Some, not content with staying at the hotel, built beautiful bungalows on the beach while others opted for massive compounds. But it was the construction of Klai Kang Won in 1926 that affirmed Hua Hin's reputation as the playground of the Royals. Klai Kang Won means 'far from worries', and that's exactly what His Majesty King Prajadhipok was hoping for when he built what is still the Royal Family's Summer Palace, which is open to the public when the Royals are not in residence.

Rivalling the Summer Palace in reputation, however, are the world-class golf courses and many internationally renowned spas that have sprung up in Hua Hin, and visitors are as likely to be seen enjoying these and the splendid beaches as taking tours of the Summer Palace.

The two Evason properties in Hua Hin are a showcase of the best that is available in Hua Hin. Both the Evason Resort & Spa and the Evason Hideaway & Spa, which are located adjacent to each other in Pranburi, 30 minutes by car south of Hua Hin, offer guests total relaxation in surroundings which make the most of their tropical environment while offering the best in modern amenities.

The Evason Resort is a large complex, with 145 rustic but luxurious guestrooms, plus 40 stand-alone private pool villas. These villas were the first of their kind to be built in Hua Hin. Scattered throughout the lush tropical gardens of the estate are all the amenities and activities your family could ask for.

Archery, tennis, sea sports, an infinity pool that's just begging to be jumped into, and shops for those in need of a little retail therapy can all be found within the Evason Resort. The holistic Six Senses Spa is a truly amazing experience, with a full range of therapeutic treatments to make you feel like a new person. Couples with children can leave the little ones at the Just Kids! Club for the whole day. The staff are adept at organising challenging

A wide palette of blues is set off by a lone coconut palm swaying in the breeze. OPPOSITE: Dusk falls over simple yet elegant table settings for a discreetly lit al fresco dinner.

activities and adventure games, doing their best to entertain the young ones while also educating them. And for parents truly in need of a night alone, supervised 'sleepovers' can be arranged by the hotel.

Guests looking for even more romantic or luxurious quarters might consider the Evason Hideaway at Hua Hin. With its 55 oversized pool villas—the smallest almost three times larger than the ones at Evason Resort—all separated by stone walls, the Evason Hideaway offers the ultimate in privacy and freedom without the fear of prying eyes. And should it be time for breakfast, an afternoon coffee or a freshly made wood-fired pizza by the pool, simply ring for your assigned butler.

Not surprisingly, many Evason Hideaway residents will probably wish to dine in their private villas. Especially popular are the in-villa barbecue dinners and Champagne breakfast—although some guests seem to have it rather late in the day. The Evason Hideaway also houses the lovely Beach Restaurant, which serves up Mediterranean fare, and The Living Room, a casual deli-style restaurant.

Additional options are available over at the Evason Resort, and guests at the Evason Hideaway are more than welcome. The two eateries, modestly named The Restaurant and The Other Restaurant, are reputed as being among the best in the area. The Restaurant is a semi-al fresco space that serves excellent Thai cuisine à la carte as well as a weekly seafood buffet. The Other Restaurant, in signature Six Senses fashion, serves imaginative fusion cuisine in an elegant yet relaxed setting. Guests can order à la carte, or can choose to try the chef's weekly 'grazing menu', a multi-course affair which truly shows off the talents of the culinary team.

From the food to the service, all the elements of a great resort are brought together, combining to create an atmosphere akin to the Royal residences of old, letting guests savour the luxury of an earlier age.

AVOCADO PICO DE GALLO PUREE CANAPES Serves 8

AVOCADO PICO DE GALLO
PUREE CANAPES
10 g / ⅜ oz butter
2 slices wheat bread, toasted
A few butter lettuce leaves
80 g / 2⅞ oz avocado flesh, chopped
20 g / ¾ oz purple onions, peeled and chopped
10 g / ⅜ oz red capsicum, chopped
10 g / ⅜ oz yellow capsicum, chopped
10 g / ⅜ oz coriander, chopped
4 tsp lemon juice
1 bird's eye chilli
Salt and pepper to taste
8 sprigs coriander for garnishing

AVOCADO PICO DE GALLO PUREE CANAPES Spread a thin layer of butter on the warm toast, then cut the toast into discs, triangles or squares with a cookie cutter. Place a small piece of lettuce on the bread. Blend the avocado, onions, capsicums, coriander, lemon juice and chilli in a food processor and work into a thick paste. Season with salt and pepper. Pour the mixture into a piping bag and pipe onto the bread pieces. Chill in refrigerator. TO SERVE Garnish the canapés with coriander.

WINE 2001 Delicato Chardonnay, Central California, USA

BRIE, WALNUT & FRUIT CANAPES Serves 8

BRIE, WALNUT & FRUIT CANAPES
20 g / ¾ oz / ¼ cup walnuts
20 g / ¾ oz butter
Salt to taste
20 g / ¾ oz butter
2 slices wheat bread, toasted
A few lollo rosso leaves
120 g / 4¼ oz Brie
Dragon fruit, cut into bite-sized pieces
Red grapes, halved, seeds removed
8 sprigs parsley for garnishing

BRIE, WALNUT & FRUIT CANAPES To caramelise the walnuts, heat butter in a non-stick pan, add the walnuts and toss to coat them. Season with salt and continue to toss until the walnuts are a rich, glossy dark brown. Drain excess oil with a piece of kitchen paper. Spread a thin layer of butter on the warm toast, then cut the toast into discs, triangles or squares with a cookie cutter. TO SERVE Place a small piece of lettuce on the bread and set a piece of cheese on it. Top this with a caramelised walnut and a piece of fresh fruit. Garnish with parsley.

WINE 2001 Delicato Chardonnay, Central California, USA

CRABMEAT & PRAWN ROE CANAPES Serves 8

CRABMEAT & PRAWN ROE CANAPES
80 g / 2⅞ oz / ⅓ cup crabmeat
40 g / 1⅜ oz mayonnaise
4 tsp vinegar
Salt and pepper to taste
20 g / ¾ oz butter
2 slices wheat bread, toasted
A few butter lettuce leaves
1 tsp prawn roe for garnishing

CRABMEAT & PRAWN ROE CANAPES Combine the crabmeat, mayonnaise and vinegar in a bowl and mix well. Season with salt and pepper. Spread a thin layer of butter on the warm toast, then cut the toast into discs, triangles or squares with a cookie cutter. TO SERVE Place a small piece of lettuce on the bread and spoon the crab mixture on it. Garnish with prawn roe.

WINE 2001 Delicato Chardonnay, Central California, USA

Roomy comfort blends with style in the split-level bar, which affords an excellent view of the Gulf of Thailand.
OPPOSITE (FROM TOP): Avocado pico de gallo purée canapés; Brie, walnut and fruit canapés; Crabmeat and prawn roe canapés.

Tangy prawn, mango and snow pea salad.
OPPOSITE: Panko-crusted salmon roll and grilled shiitake mushrooms with Asian chipotle vinaigrette.

TANGY PRAWN, MANGO & SNOW PEA SALAD Serves 2

DRESSING
2 tsp Dijon mustard
2 tsp rice wine vinegar
4 tsp corn oil
Salt and pepper, to taste
TANGY PRAWN, MANGO & SNOW PEA SALAD
120 g / 4¼ oz snow pea pods, blanched
Oil for frying
50 g / 1¾ oz red onion, peeled and sliced
Thumb-sized piece of ginger, peeled and cut into thin strips
2 tsp sambal oelek
360 g / 12½ oz large prawns, peeled and deveined
Juice from 2 limes
200 g / 7 oz mango, diced
Salt and pepper to taste
Mango slices for garnishing

DRESSING In a mixing bowl, whisk together the mustard, vinegar and oil. Season with salt and pepper. TANGY PRAWN, MANGO & SNOW PEA SALAD Toss the snow peas with the dressing and set aside. In a hot wok, caramelise the onions and ginger in oil. Add the sambal and prawns and stir-fry until just cooked. Deglaze with the lime juice and add the mango. Adjust seasoning to taste. TO SERVE Place a portion of snow peas in the centre of a plate. Surround it with stir-fried prawns. Garnish with mango slices.

WINE 1999 Sancerre Cuvée Edmond, Alphonse Mellot, France

PANKO-CRUSTED SALMON ROLL & GRILLED SHIITAKE MUSHROOMS WITH ASIAN CHIPOTLE VINAIGRETTE Serves 2

SALMON ROLL
300 g / 10½ oz centre-cut salmon fillet, cut into 2 portions, pounded flat (paillarde) and grilled
2 sheets nori
200 g / 7 oz / 2 cups cooked sushi rice
Salt and pepper to taste
PANKO CRUST
60 g / 2⅛ oz / ½ cup cornstarch
1 egg, beaten with a little water
30 g / 1 oz / 1 cup panko or breadcrumbs
Corn oil for frying
ASIAN CHIPOTLE VINAIGRETTE
2 shallots, peeled and coarsely chopped
5 tsp tamari soy sauce
Juice from 2 limes
2 chipotle chillies (canned in adobo sauce)
5 tsp extra virgin olive oil
Wasabi powder and salt to taste
GRILLED SHIITAKE MUSHROOMS
8 shiitake mushroom caps
1 tbsp vinaigrette
100 g / 3½ oz fennel bulb, shaved thinly and soaked in iced water for garnishing

SALMON ROLL Place a portion of grilled salmon at one end of a nori sheet lying on a bamboo sushi mat. Place half the sushi rice in a strip above the salmon, leaving the top end of the nori empty. Starting with the bottom end, roll up tightly. Moisten the end of the nori and press firmly to seal the roll. Let it rest on the sealed edge for 5 minutes. Prepare 2 rolls. PANKO CRUST Place the cornstarch, beaten egg and panko in 3 separate containers. Dredge the sushi rolls in the cornstarch, followed by the beaten egg and finally the panko. Deep-fry for 4 to 6 minutes until golden brown. Drain the rolls on kitchen paper. ASIAN CHIPOTLE VINAIGRETTE Process the shallots, tamari, lime juice and chipotle chillies in a blender. Slowly incorporate the olive oil until emulsified. Season with wasabi powder and salt. GRILLED SHIITAKE MUSHROOMS Grill the shiitake mushrooms. If the tops are very round, slice them off to create a flat surface before grilling. Toss the grilled mushrooms with a little vinaigrette and set aside. TO SERVE Arrange 4 grilled mushrooms in the centre of a plate. Cut a sushi roll in half, and slice each half diagonally. Put each piece of sushi roll on a grilled mushroom and garnish with fennel. Drizzle some vinaigrette over.

WINE 1999 Marrowbone Chardonnay, Saddler's Creek Winery, Hunter Valley, Australia

WOK-SEARED PEPPER PRAWNS WITH LEMON JASMINE RICE Serves 2

LEMON JASMINE RICE
4 stalks spring onions, white and green portions separated and finely chopped
Zest and juice from ½ lemon
1½ tsp corn oil
200 g / 7 oz / 1 cup jasmine rice, rinsed until water runs clear
Thumb-sized piece of ginger, peeled and sliced
Salt and ground white pepper to taste
300 ml / 10⅛ fl oz / 1¼ cups chicken stock (see Basics)
WOK-SEARED PRAWNS
380 g / 13¼ oz prawns, shells removed and deveined
½ tsp ground black pepper
1 tsp ground white pepper
A pinch of ground Szechuan pepper
1 tsp salt
4 tsp cornstarch
4 stalks spring onions (green part only), finely chopped
4 tsp corn oil
2 sprigs parsley for garnishing
Thin slices of lime or lemon for garnishing

LEMON JASMINE RICE In a hot pan, sauté the spring onions and lemon zest with a little oil. Add the rice and ginger and sauté a further 3 minutes. Add the salt, pepper, lemon juice and chicken stock. Cover and bring to a boil. Reduce heat and simmer for 15 to 20 minutes. Remove from heat and allow to stand, covered, for a further 25 minutes. WOK-SEARED PRAWNS Soak the prawns in cold salted water for 20 minutes then rinse well. In a separate bowl, combine the pepper, salt and cornstarch. Dredge the prawns through this mixture, then quickly fry them in very hot oil. Add the spring onions and cook for about 3 to 5 minutes until the prawns are pink. TO SERVE Pack a portion of rice into a ring mould placed on a plate. Remove mould and set half the prawns on the rice. Garnish with parsley and citrus slices.

WINE 2000 Château de Campuget, Costières de Nimes, France

THAI BASIL ICE CREAM WITH FRUIT COMPOTE Serves 2

THAI BASIL ICE CREAM
500 ml / 17 fl oz / 2⅛ cups milk
25 g / ⅞ oz Thai basil leaves
5 g / ⅛ oz mint leaves
½ vanilla pod, split lengthwise and scraped for seeds
100 g / 3½ oz / ⅜ cup sugar
6 egg yolks
220 ml / 7½ fl oz / 1 cup heavy cream
FRUIT COMPOTE
80 g / 2⅞ oz pineapple, peeled and diced
100 g / 3½ oz mango, peeled and diced
80 g / 2⅞ oz papaya, peeled and diced
50 ml / 1¾ fl oz / ¼ cup Beaum de Venise, or other sweet dessert wine
2 sprigs mint for garnishing

THAI BASIL ICE CREAM In a saucepan, simmer the milk at just under a boil with the basil, mint and vanilla pod and seeds to reduce by half. Steep in the refrigerator overnight. Strain out the herbs and vanilla pod before reheating it to a boil and adding the sugar. Stir until sugar dissolves. Remove from heat. Hand-whisk the yolks in a mixing bowl. Temper the yolks by adding 1 ladleful of the hot milk to it and mixing well. Then add the yolk mixture to the rest of the hot milk and whisk continuously for 2 minutes. Add the cream and mix well. Place the mixture in an ice bath until completely cool. Transfer to an ice cream maker and process according to the manufacturer's instructions. FRUIT COMPOTE Heat all the ingredients in a non-stick pan. Reduce the liquid by 20 percent, when the fruit should be cooked yet firm to the bite. TO SERVE Ladle the fruit compôte into a chilled bowl. Top with a scoop of the ice cream and garnish with a mint sprig.

WINE Miranda du Golden Botrytis, Riverina, King Valley, Australia

Warm brown hues of natural wood surround the private pool of the pool villa, which gives guests unrivalled privacy and exclusivity.
OPPOSITE (FROM REAR): Thai basil ice cream with fruit compôte; Wok-seared pepper prawns with lemon jasmine rice.

The bright, airy room opens out to the inviting turquoise of the private pool. OPPOSITE (FROM LEFT): Sweet potato risotto with seared scallops and mushrooms with green bean salad; Dijon-marinated lamb with Thai ratatouille; Caramelised lemon tart.

SWEET POTATO RISOTTO WITH SEARED SCALLOPS & MUSHROOMS Serves 2

SWEET POTATO RISOTTO
50 g / 1¾ oz shallots, peeled and finely diced
2 tsp unsalted butter
Salt and pepper to taste
500 g / 1 lb 1 oz sweet potato, finely diced
500 ml / 17 fl oz / 2⅛ cups hot chicken stock (see Basics)
SEARED SCALLOPS & MUSHROOMS
500 g / 1 lb 1⅝ oz / 2½ cups scallops
Salt and pepper to taste
Oil for frying
1 tsp minced garlic
½ tsp minced ginger
200 g / 7 oz / 1½ cups straw mushrooms
Salt and pepper to taste
GREEN BEAN SALAD
Juice from 1 lemon
1 tsp truffle oil
40 ml / 1⅜ fl oz / ¼ cup extra virgin olive oil
Salt and pepper to taste
220 g / 8⅛ oz / 2 cups green beans, trimmed, blanched and refreshed
5 g / ⅛ oz chives, cut into 2.5-cm / 1-inch sticks
Truffle oil for garnishing

SWEET POTATO RISOTTO Sauté the shallots in butter and season lightly. Add the sweet potato and sauté. Add 1 ladleful of the hot stock and stir until it is fully absorbed before adding the next ladleful. Continue this way until the mixture is creamy, not mushy. SEARED SCALLOPS & MUSHROOMS Season the scallops and sauté in a very hot pan coated with oil for 6 to 8 minutes until both sides are brown. Remove. Wipe the pan and re-heat with more oil. Sauté the garlic and ginger until soft then add the mushrooms. Season and cook for a further 6 to 8 minutes. Set aside. GREEN BEAN SALAD Mix the lemon juice, truffle oil, olive oil and seasoning. Toss with the blanched green beans. Adjust seasoning and add the chives. TO SERVE Place a ring mould in the centre of a plate and fill half with mushrooms. Top with risotto and press gently. Remove the ring. Top with green bean salad and surround with scallops. Garnish with chives and truffle oil.

WINE 1999 Domaine Leon Beyer Gewürztraminer, Alsace, France

DIJON MARINATED LAMB WITH THAI RATATOUILLE Serves 2

DIJON MARINATED LAMB
200 g / 7 oz lamb rack, fat and silverskin removed
2 tbsp red wine (Californian zinfandel or pinot noir)
2 tbsp Dijon mustard
2 tsp dried thyme
2 tsp minced garlic
4 tsp tamari soy sauce
2 tsp corn oil
Salt and pepper to taste
THAI RATATOUILLE
5 stalks spring onions, sliced thinly
Thumb-sized piece of ginger, peeled and sliced
5 cloves garlic, peeled and sliced thinly
½ tbsp fermented black beans, rinsed
1 tbsp olive oil
40 g / 1⅜ oz Japanese eggplant, diced
40 g / 1⅜ oz tomatoes, diced
40 g / 1⅜ oz zucchini, diced
A few Thai basil leaves, cut into thin strips
A few kaffir lime leaves, cut into thin strips
1 tsp fish sauce
Juice from 2 limes
Salt to taste
CORIANDER TAPENADE
1 clove garlic, peeled
40 g / 1⅜ oz Niçoise olives, pitted
12 g / ⅜ oz coriander
5 g / ⅛ oz mint
Extra virgin olive oil for emulsifying
Salt to taste
A few sprigs of coriander for garnishing

DIJON MARINATED LAMB Marinate the lamb in the remaining ingredients for at least 2 hours. Preheat oven to 170°C / 340°F. Pan-fry the lamb in oil over medium heat until it begins to brown, then roast in oven for 20 to 25 minutes for medium rare. THAI RATATOUILLE Sauté the spring onions, garlic, ginger and black beans in olive oil for 2 minutes. Add eggplant and sauté for 2 minutes. Add tomatoes and zucchini. Reduce heat and simmer for 20 to 25 minutes until zucchini is tender. Add basil, lime leaves, fish sauce, lime juice and seasoning. CORIANDER TAPENADE Crush all the ingredients except salt together with a mortar and pestle. Season. TO SERVE Place some ratatouille on a plate and arrange evenly cut lamb medallions around. Top with tapenade and coriander.

WINE 2000 Revereto Gavi del Commune di Gavi, Michele Chiarlo, Piedmont, Italy

CARAMELISED LEMON TART

Serves 2

SHORT CRUST DOUGH
40 g / 1⅜ oz / ⅓ cup plain flour
2½ tbsp unsalted butter, diced
3 tbsp icing sugar, sifted
A pinch of salt
1 egg yolk
1 tsp lemon zest
EGG WASH
1 egg yolk
2 tbsp water
LEMON FILLING
Zest and juice from 1 lemon
60 ml / 2 fl oz / ¼ cup heavy cream
2 eggs
6 tbsp sugar
Icing sugar for dusting

SHORT CRUST DOUGH Sift the flour onto a work surface and make a well in the centre. Place butter cubes in the well and work with fingertips until soft. Sift icing sugar over the butter, add the salt and work into the butter. Add the egg yolk and mix well. Gradually draw in the flour and mix thoroughly. Rub lemon zest into the dough (do not overwork as the dough will become elastic). Roll the dough out between 2 sheets of grease-proof paper and refrigerate for at least 2 hours before use. The tart shells must be blind baked (pre-baked without filling). Preheat oven to 200°C / 400°F. Butter a baking ring and refrigerate for 10 minutes. On a lightly floured surface, roll the chilled dough out to about 0.6 cm / 0.25 inch thick and place it over the baking ring. Press into the sides gently, allowing some of the dough to overhang. Chill in the fridge for 10 minutes. Line the dough with greaseproof paper and fill with baking beans. Bake for 2 minutes then remove from oven and remove the beans. Check the tart for cracks or holes. EGG WASH Mix the yolk with water. Brush the crust with the egg wash and return to the oven to glaze slightly. Once glazed, remove and allow to cool. LEMON FILLING Strain the lemon juice. In a bowl, whip the cream until it thickens to the ribbon stage. Break the eggs into a separate bowl and add the sugar. Whisk until smooth and well blended. Stir in the lemon zest and juice, then whisk in the cream. Allow to steep in refrigerator for at least 1 hour before passing through a fine-mesh sieve. Pour the filling into the pre-baked shell and bake for 40 to 60 minutes at 140°C / 285°F. After 40 minutes, check frequently as the filling should just be setting. When cooked, remove from oven. Allow to cool for at least 4 hours before cutting. TO SERVE Cut the tart into wedges. Dust with icing sugar and caramelise the sugar with a blowtorch.

WINE 1999 St Helena, Late Harvest, Canterbury, New Zealand

CITRUS & JICAMA SOM TAM WITH GRILLED PRAWNS Serves 2

DRESSING
200 ml / 6¾ fl oz / ⅞ cup fresh orange juice
1 tsp Dijon mustard
1½ tsp soy sauce
2 tsp rice vinegar
10 g / ⅜ oz shallots, peeled and minced
1½ tsp olive oil
Salt and black pepper to taste
CITRUS & JICAMA SOM TAM
80 g / 2⅞ oz jicama, peeled and finely sliced
40 g / 1⅜ oz cucumber, finely sliced
Salt and black pepper to taste
GRILLED PRAWNS
4 stalks spring onion, sliced
Olive oil for frying
200 g / 7 oz prawns, peeled and deveined
Salt and black pepper to taste
40 g / 1⅜ oz navel orange segments
20 g / ¾ oz grapefruit segments
20 g / ¾ oz lime segments
20 g / ¾ oz lemon segments

DRESSING In a saucepan, reduce the orange juice to a thick syrupy consistency. Remove from heat and set aside. In a separate bowl whisk together the Dijon, soy sauce, rice vinegar, shallots and olive oil. Season with salt and pepper. CITRUS & JICAMA SOM TAM Toss and coat the jicama in the dressing. Coat the cucumber with the remainder. Adjust seasoning to taste. Line a mould about 5 cm / 2 inches high and 7.5 cm / 3 inches in diameter with the cucumbers and fill with the coated jicama. GRILLED PRAWNS In another pan, caramelise the spring onions in olive oil. Add the prawns, season and cook for about 4 to 5 minutes. Add all the citrus segments and cook for about 1 minute to warm them. Adjust seasoning. TO SERVE Place the prawns over the jicama, remove the mould and drizzle the reduced orange juice around the prawns.

WINE 1999 Yarden Galilee Sauvignon Blanc, Golan Heights, Israel

CRISPY SKINNED SALMON, MASHED POTATO & MESCLUN SALAD WITH SAFFRON-PEPPER JUS Serves 2

CRISPY SKINNED SALMON
1 tsp soy sauce
1 tsp red wine vinegar
200 g / 7 oz salmon fillet with skin, bones and fat removed, and cut into 2 portions
MASHED POTATO
100 g / 3½ oz potatoes, boiled, peeled and grated
50 ml / 1¾ fl oz / ¼ cup low fat milk, warmed
2 tsp butter
Salt and pepper to taste
DRESSING
2 tbsp soy sauce
1 tbsp sesame oil
2 tsp lemon juice
MESCLUN SALAD
120 g / 4¼ oz mesclun salad mix (endive, lamb's lettuce, dandelion, rocket, oakleaf lettuce and mixed herbs)
10 g / ⅜ oz fresh basil, shredded
15 g / ½ oz shallots, peeled and sliced
SAFFRON-PEPPER JUS
40 g / 1⅜ oz shiitake mushrooms, cut into thin strips
Oil for frying
50 ml / 1¾ fl oz / ¼ cup chicken stock (see Basics)
A pinch of saffron
40 ml / 1⅜ fl oz / ¼ cup extra virgin olive oil
2 tsp balsamic vinegar
40 g / 1⅜ oz tomatoes, finely diced
1 tbsp black peppercorns, cracked

CRISPY SKINNED SALMON Mix the soy sauce and vinegar, and brush it over the salmon, skin side only. Broil on high heat for about 6 to 7 minutes. Set aside. MASHED POTATO Put the grated potato into a saucepan and slowly add the warm milk, stirring constantly to maintain a smooth mixture. Warm gently, then add the butter. When melted, season and set aside. Keep warm. DRESSING Mix the soy sauce, sesame oil and lemon juice. Set aside. MESCLUN SALAD Combine the salad leaves with the basil and shallots. Pour the dressing over and toss well. SAFFRON-PEPPER JUS In a pan, sauté the mushrooms in oil over high heat. Set aside. Warm the chicken stock, add the saffron and cook for about 10 minutes. Add the olive oil, balsamic vinegar, tomatoes, peppercorns and mushrooms. Mix gently and season to taste. TO SERVE Place the mashed potatoes in the centre of a warm serving plate. Arrange the salmon on top, spoon the sauce around and garnish with the salad.

WINE 1996 LA Cetto, Reserva Limitada, Nebbiolo, Valle de Guadalupe, Baja California, Mexico

PUMPKIN CUSTARD

Serves 2

PUMPKIN CUSTARD
2 eggs
2 egg yolks
150 ml / 5 fl oz / ⅝ cup coconut milk
150 g / 5¼ oz grated palm sugar
2½ tbsp potato flour
2 small pumpkins, hollowed out into bowls
Fried buckwheat noodles for garnishing

PUMPKIN CUSTARD Preheat oven to 180°C / 350°F. Combine all ingredients, making sure the sugar is completely dissolved before pouring the mixture into small pumpkins. Place some water on an oven-proof tray. Place the pumpkins on an oven-proof dish and place this on the tray with water. Bake in the oven until the custard is set and the pumpkin is soft yet able to hold its shape. When cooked, remove from oven and let cool to room temperature before chilling. TO SERVE Present pumpkin custard on a chilled plate, garnished with fried buckwheat noodles.

WINE 2000 De Bortoli's Sacred Hill Traminer Riesling, New South Wales, Australia

Rustic wooden walkways lead to villas which are set in the midst of abundant tropical greenery.
OPPOSITE (FROM LEFT): Citrus and jicama som tam with grilled prawns; Crispy skinned salmon, mashed potato and mesclun salad with saffron-pepper jus; Pumpkin custard.

RED DUCK CURRY Serves 4

RED DUCK CURRY
50 g / 1¾ oz Thai red curry paste
800 ml / 1 pt 7 fl oz / 3⅓ cups coconut cream
200 g / 7 oz pineapple, peeled and diced
100 g / 3½ oz red grapes
100 g / 3½ oz green grapes
16 cherry tomatoes
100 g / 3½ oz young eggplant
100 g / 3½ oz eggplant, sliced and quartered
10 g / ⅜ oz basil, cut into thin strips
20 kaffir lime leaves
2 large red chillies, seeded and sliced
4 tsp Thai fish sauce
4 tsp grated palm sugar
Salt to taste
400 g / 14⅛ oz Chinese roast duck, with bones,
cut into bite-sized pieces
4 tsp coconut cream

RED DUCK CURRY Heat the curry paste until fragrant. Add the coconut cream and bring to a boil to fully dissolve the paste. Add all the remaining ingredients except the duck and bring to a boil again. Cook for about 5 minutes then add the duck and mix well. Continue to heat until well warmed. TO SERVE Transfer curry to warm bowls and garnish with a little coconut cream.

Rectangles of light set in white stuccoed walls illuminate a walkway. OPPOSITE (CLOCKWISE FROM LEFT): Red duck curry; Stir-fried lobster with garlic and pepper; Fruit salad; Coconut soup with prawns; Thai vegetable crudités with dip; Mango and sticky rice.

STIR-FRIED LOBSTER WITH GARLIC & PEPPER Serves 4

STIR-FRIED LOBSTER WITH GARLIC & PEPPER
100 g / 3½ oz garlic, peeled and minced
2 tsp coarsely ground black pepper
Vegetable oil for frying
4 lobster tails, shells removed and cut into 2- to
3- cm / 0.8- to 1.2-inch pieces
4 tsp soy sauce
4 tsp oyster sauce
400 ml / 13½ fl oz / 1⅔ cups chicken stock
(see Basics)
Deep-fried sliced garlic for garnishing

STIR-FRIED LOBSTER WITH GARLIC & PEPPER In a hot wok, fry the garlic and pepper in oil until fragrant. Add the lobster meat, soy sauce, oyster sauce and just enough chicken stock to maintain desired consistency of sauce. When the lobster is cooked, adjust the seasoning. TO SERVE Garnish with deep-fried garlic.

FRUIT SALAD Serves 4

FRUIT SALAD
100 g / 3½ oz grapes
1 red apple
1 green apple
100 g / 3½ oz cantaloupe
1 rose apple
100 g / 3½ oz pineapple
Salt, sugar and bird's eye chilli to taste

FRUIT SALAD Cut all the fruit into bite-sized pieces and combine in a mixing bowl. Season to taste. TO SERVE Serve in a chilled bowl.

MANGO & STICKY RICE Serves 4

MANGO & STICKY RICE
400 g / 14⅛ oz uncooked glutinous rice
100 ml / 3⅜ fl oz / ⅜ cup coconut milk
80 g / 2⅞ oz / ⅓ cup sugar
1 tsp salt
2 fresh mangoes, peeled and sliced

MANGO & STICKY RICE Soak the glutinous rice in water for 5 hours. Drain, rinse and steam for 15 to 20 minutes until nearly cooked. Combine the coconut milk, sugar and salt in a separate pan and bring to a boil, stirring often. Reduce to a simmer. When the rice is ready, remove from the steamer and fold into the warm coconut milk mixture. Mix well for the rice to finish cooking in the coconut milk. It is done when the rice is cooked and the coconut milk has been absorbed. Let cool. TO SERVE Arrange half a mango on each plate and serve with a portion of rice.

COCONUT SOUP WITH PRAWNS Serves 4

COCONUT SOUP WITH PRAWNS
600 ml / 1 pt 1¼ fl oz / 2½ cups coconut cream
200 ml / 6¾ fl oz / ⅞ cup chicken stock (see Basics)
100 g / 3½ oz lemon grass, washed and sliced
20 kaffir lime leaves, cut into thin strips
200 g / 7 oz galangal, peeled and sliced
200 g / 7 oz / 1½ cups straw mushrooms
8 large prawns, shells removed with heads intact
and deveined
4 bird's eye chillies
4 tbsp lime juice or to taste
½ tsp fish sauce or to taste
Salt and sugar to taste
A few kaffir lime leaves for garnishing

COCONUT SOUP WITH PRAWNS In a pan, heat and reduce the coconut cream to desired thickness. Use the chicken stock to balance the consistency during the cooking process. Add the herbs and mushrooms and cook for 5 minutes, then add the prawns, chillies and seasoning. Heat until the prawns are just cooked. Check seasoning. TO SERVE Ladle soup into a warm soup bowl. Place 2 prawns on top. Garnish with lime leaves.

THAI VEGETABLE CRUDITES WITH DIP Serves 4

DIP
200 ml / 6¾ fl oz / ⅞ cup chicken stock
(see Basics)
100 g / 3½ oz prawn paste
60 g / 2⅛ oz / ¾ cup dried prawns, soaked in hot
water for 15 minutes and rinsed
60 g / 2⅛ oz shallots, peeled and chopped
12 cloves garlic, peeled
Thai bird's eye chillies to taste
4 tbsp Thai fish sauce
4 tsp lime juice
Palm sugar to taste
VEGETABLE CRUDITES
60 g / 2⅛ oz long beans, cut into 10-cm /
4-inch segments
8 wing bean pods
8 young corns
60 g / 2⅛ oz cucumber, peeled and sliced
8 Thai eggplants
60 g / 2⅛ oz asparagus, cut into 10-cm / 4-inch
segments with tips
1 white cabbage, quartered

DIP Process all the ingredients in a blender to get a thick paste. Adjust seasoning to taste. VEGETABLE CRUDITES Prepare vegetables as recommended. TO SERVE Arrange the prepared vegetables around a bowl of dip on a serving platter.

POT STICKERS Serves 2

POT STICKERS
30 g / 1 oz red onion, peeled and sliced
Thumb-sized piece of ginger, peeled and minced
Oil for frying
25 g / ⅞ oz shiitake mushrooms, sliced
25 g / ⅞ oz cabbage, shredded
25 g / ⅞ oz carrot, shredded
25 g / ⅞ oz garlic chives, chopped
Salt and pepper to taste
½ tsp sesame oil
10 g / ⅜ oz coriander, chopped
8 gyoza wrappers or wonton skin
Corn oil for frying
60 ml / 2 fl oz / ¼ cup water
SPICY SOY DIPPING SAUCE
1 tbsp light soy sauce
1 tbsp rice wine vinegar
4 stalks spring onions, chopped
1 tbsp sesame oil
1 tbsp sambal
Salad leaves of your choice for garnishing

POT STICKERS Sauté the onions and ginger in a little oil. Add the mushrooms and stir. Add the cabbage, carrots and chives. Season with salt and pepper. Cook until the mixture is soft then transfer to a colander to drain excess juices and oil. When cool, add the sesame oil and coriander and mix well. Check and adjust seasoning. Place 1 to 2 tsp of the mixture on round gyoza wrappers and fold to make half moon dumplings with flat bottoms. Place dumplings into a hot pan coated with oil. When the dumpling bottoms brown, add the water and cover immediately to steam. Steam until the water has completely evaporated and the bottoms get crispy again. SPICY SOY DIPPING SAUCE Mix all the ingredients and adjust seasoning to taste. TO SERVE Arrange in a serving dish with salad leaves, accompanied by a saucer of the dipping sauce.

WINE Concha y Toro Frontera Chardonnay, Central Valley, Chile

GRILLED VEGETABLE PAELLA WITH BASIL TOMATO SLAW

Serves 2

GRILLED VEGETABLES
30 g / 1 oz zucchini, cut into long strips
30 g / 1 oz eggplant, cut into long strips
30 g / 1 oz red capsicum, cut into long strips
30 g / 1 oz yellow capsicum, cut into long strips
30 g / 1 oz red onion, peeled and cut into wedges
PAELLA
300 g / 10½ oz / 1½ cups uncooked basmati rice
30 g / 1 oz shallots, peeled and minced
2 cloves garlic, peeled and minced
Thumb-sized piece of ginger, peeled and minced
Olive oil for frying
Salt and pepper to taste
A pinch of turmeric
500 ml / 17 fl oz / 2 cups vegetable stock
(see Basics)
BASIL TOMATO SLAW
15 g / ½ oz Thai basil, cut into thin strips
60 g / 2⅛ oz tomatoes, seeds removed and cut into thin strips
30 g / 1 oz red onion, peeled and sliced
2½ tsp balsamic vinegar
1 tsp black vinegar
2 tbsp extra virgin olive oil
Salt and pepper to taste
Salad leaves of your choice for garnishing

GRILLED VEGETABLES Grill the vegetables in a greased pan for 15 minutes or until softened. Allow to cool then cut into 1.2-cm / 0.5-inch cubes. PAELLA Sauté the rice, shallots, garlic and ginger for 4 to 6 minutes in an oven-proof pan brushed with olive oil. Season, add the turmeric and stir a further 2 minutes. Add the stock and grilled vegetable cubes. Cover and bake at 180°C / 350°F for 1 hour or until the rice has completely absorbed the stock. Fluff the rice with a fork and adjust the seasoning. BASIL TOMATO SLAW Mix all the ingredients and season to taste. Set aside. TO SERVE Scoop the paella into warm serving dishes with the tomato slaw sprinkled over the top. Garnish with salad leaves.

WINE Concha y Toro Frontera Chardonnay, Central Valley, Chile

PANKO AND MACADAMIA-CRUSTED BANANA SPRING ROLLS Serves 2

PANKO AND MACADAMIA-CRUSTED BANANA SPRING ROLLS
2 bananas, peeled and quartered
8 wonton skins
100 g / 3½ oz / ⅔ cup cake flour
100 g / 3½ oz / 2⅞ cups panko or breadcrumbs
100 g / 3½ oz / 1 cup macadamia nuts, chopped
2 eggs
Oil for frying

PANKO AND MACADAMIA-CRUSTED BANANA SPRING ROLLS Wrap each banana in wonton skins like a spring roll. Roll in flour and shake off excess. Mix the panko and macadamia nuts together in a separate bowl. In another bowl, beat eggs well and add just a few drops of water. Dip the spring rolls in the beaten egg, then dredge in the panko and macadamia mixture. Deep-fry in hot oil until the rolls begin to brown. TO SERVE Arrange rolls in a serving dish and serve hot.

WINE Concha y Toro Frontera Chardonnay, Central Valley, Chile

Lily pads float tranquilly on the surface of a pond in the garden.
OPPOSITE (FROM LEFT): Pot stickers; Grilled vegetable paella with basil tomato slaw; Panko and macadamia-crusted banana spring rolls.

TOFU & SPINACH SALAD WITH SPICY MISO DRESSING

Serves 2

SPICY MISO DRESSING
4 tsp rice wine vinegar
1½ tsp light soy sauce
30 g / 1 oz miso paste
1½ tsp sambal oelek
½ tsp sugar
25 g / ⅞ oz pickled ginger, chopped
1½ tsp sesame oil
3 tbsp corn oil
Salt and white pepper to taste
SPINACH SALAD
5 stalks spring onions (green part only), chopped
40 g / 1⅜ oz spinach, cut into thin strips
200 g / 7 oz egg tofu, sliced
1 tsp toasted sesame seeds for garnishing

SPICY MISO DRESSING Process the vinegar, soy, miso, sambal, sugar and pickled ginger in a blender until smooth. Slowly drizzle both oils in and process to a fine emulsion. Check and balance the seasoning. SPINACH SALAD Transfer the dressing into a bowl and add the spring onions. Toss the spinach with the dressing. TO SERVE Arrange layers of spinach and tofu in 2 glass serving dishes. Garnish with the remaining dressing and sesame seeds.

WINE 2000 Fiddler's Green Riesling, Waipara, New Zealand

WOK-SEARED LOBSTER WITH MANGO Serves 2

WOK-SEARED LOBSTER WITH MANGO
3 cloves garlic, peeled and sliced thinly
1 goat pepper, stemmed and chopped
10 g / ⅜ oz spring onions (green part only), minced
2 tsp coconut oil
200 g / 7 oz lobster, head removed, tail cut into
4 pieces, claw shells cracked
80 g / 2⅞ oz mango flesh, cut into 1.2-cm / 0.5-inch cubes
20 g / ¾ oz snow peas
2 tbsp Malibu rum
500 ml / 17 fl oz / 2⅛ cups seafood stock (see Basics)
10 g / ⅜ oz unsalted butter
Salt and pepper to taste
A few sprigs of parsley for garnishing

WOK-SEARED LOBSTER WITH MANGO In a hot wok, sauté the garlic, goat pepper and onions in the coconut oil for 2 minutes or until soft. Add the lobster. When lobster is evenly seared, add the mango and peas and mix well. Add the rum and flambé before reducing the liquid by half. Pour in the seafood stock and reduce the mixture by a quarter. Add the butter and continue to cook until lobster is done. Adjust the seasoning. TO SERVE Divide the mixture between 2 glass serving dishes and garnish with parsley sprigs.

WINE 1994 Königschaffhausen Hasenberg Ruländer Beerenauslese, Baden, Germany

FRESH SLICED TROPICAL FRUIT WITH CITRUS SORBET

Serves 2

FRESH SLICED TROPICAL FRUIT
100 g / 3½ oz watermelon, peeled and diced
100 g / 3½ oz papaya, peeled and diced
100 g / 3½ oz pineapple, peeled and diced
100 g / 3½ oz honeydew melon, peeled and diced
CITRUS SORBET
2 scoops sorbet, any citrus flavour
2 sprigs of mint for garnishing

FRESH SLICED TROPICAL FRUIT Mix all the fruit together in a mixing bowl. TO SERVE Divide the fruit between 2 glass serving dishes. Top with a scoop of sorbet and garnish with mint.

WINE 2000 Elysium Black Muscat, Andrew Quady, Madera, California, USA

The sea stretches from the foot of your deckchair to the horizon beyond.
OPPOSITE (FROM LEFT): Tofu and spinach salad with spicy miso dressing; Wok-seared lobster with mango; Fresh sliced tropical fruit with citrus sorbet.

ANA MANDARA, the luxurious Evason retreat in Vietnam, was significantly brought to the world's attention in the pages of Sports Illustrated's 2003 Swimsuit Edition. Hovering in the background, the romantic, tropical backdrop to the pictures sufficiently piqued the imagination of readers such that the Ana Mandara website was flooded by hits, which subsequently translated into an overwhelming increase in the resort's occupancy.

Ana Mandara, located on the beach of Nha Trang, the coastal capital of Vietnam's Khanh Hoa province, offers an abundance of natural beauty to discover. There's 200 kilometres (approximately 124 miles) of sandy coastline here, with over 200 tiny islands dotting the crystalline waters. Nha Trang's beaches are reputed to be Vietnam's best, and the scuba diving and snorkelling world-class. The climate is exceptional as well. While the southern part of the country (including Ho Chi Minh City) is being pummelled by summer monsoons, Nha Trang is sunny and fair, making it an excellent summer vacation destination. In fact, except for the two-month rainy season—mid-October to mid-December—Nha Trang is gorgeous all year round.

However, there's more to Nha Trang than the sun and sand. The area is rich in culture and history, and tourists can visit the Cham Po Nagar temple complex, built between the 8th and 13th centuries, and the Long Son Pagoda. The pagoda was first built at the base of a hill in 1886, but had to be rebuilt after storm damage in 1900. The White Buddha on the top of the slope was erected in 1963 in memory of the monks and nuns who rose in valiant protest against the Diem regime.

To the west of the pagoda lie the ruins of Dien Khanh citadel, which was built in 1793 under the Nguyen Anh dynasty. It covers an impressive area of 36 square kilometres (approximately 14 square miles) and is surrounded by four moats. It was a military and residential complex, and had previously housed a palace, warehouses and jails. The second-oldest citadel in Vietnam, it is a change from the lighter pursuits that can be found in the surrounding areas.

More active visitors will love island-hopping among the many emerald islands that dot the waters here. One of the most popular destinations is Hon Mieu island, where an incredibly inventive fisherman named Le Can built a unique aquarium with three seawater ponds, each containing a microcosm of the area's marine life. Visiting the Tri Nguyen Aquarium and seeing the range of fish, sharks and the other underwater creatures there is a simply breathtaking experience.

After a long day spent swimming around these islands, there is no better prospect than returning to the luxurious Ana Mandara. Ana Mandara—which means 'beautiful home for guests' in Cham, the language of the Champa kingdom which ruled central and southern Vietnam from 192 CE to 1697—has been built to evoke the spirit of an old Vietnamese village, albeit one with six-star service and amenities.

Waves lap gently at the sandy beach, in full view of Ana Mandara.
OPPOSITE: Sticks of incense on the ground hint at the adherence to tradition that prevails; the Six Senses Spa pavilions are ideal places to relax and savour the resort's idyllic charm.

Spread across 2.6 hectares (approximately 6.4 acres) of tropical gardens overlooking the sea, the resort offers 74 guest rooms ranging in size from 27 to 42 square metres (approximately 290 to 452 square feet), housed in 16 villas.

You can rest your tired body in your room, but we recommend a visit to the Six Senses Spa, where the treatments are sure to rejuvenate you. As in all Six Senses Spas, the spa at Ana Mandara specialises in holistic treatments which refresh and revive. After a session of pampering, it's high time for dinner.

Guests can dine by the beach or in the main restaurant. Vietnamese cuisine is as rich as its culture. Try phở—Vietnam's famous beef noodle soup—or fresh summer rolls. The chefs have also come up with an exciting Western menu, which boasts roast chicken, rack of lamb and barbecued seafood. And of course, no visit to any Six Senses resort is complete without sampling something from Six Senses' trademark fusion menu. Here at Ana Mandara, where Asian and European cultures and cuisines have intermingled for generations, you'll find the fusion cuisine to be truly delectable, with a touch of refined subtlety.

Those who have enjoyed their stays at Ana Mandara will soon find themselves with two more reasons to revisit Vietnam. The first is Evason Hideaway at Ana Mandara, which, as in other Evason Hideaways, provides guests with an exclusive private villa experience. It is located in a secluded bay accessible only by boat, and the trip is 15 minutes from Ana Mandara Resort. The 53 villas—all with private pools—range in size from 154 to 271 square metres (approximately 1,658 to 2,917 square feet). Slightly further away, Ana Mandara has found a new home in Dalat with Ana Mandara Villas Dalat. Fifteen restored French colonial villas now make up a beautiful new resort with 42 rooms. The Shivdasanis' commitment to luxury, heritage and the environment can be seen at its best in Ana Mandara, where the antique and modern are inimitably fused together.

The infinity pool seems to extend interminably and meld seamlessly with the sea and land beyond.
OPPOSITE (FROM TOP): Wild mushroom frittata with roasted cherry tomato salad; Tempura of China Sea anchovies on daikon and seaweed purée; Tea-smoked salmon on grilled sweet potato.

TEA-SMOKED SALMON ON GRILLED SWEET POTATO

Serves 8

TEA-SMOKED SALMON
3 tbsp tea leaves of your choice
60 g / 2⅛ oz / ½ cup sawdust of untreated wood
1 tsp orange zest
2 tsp lemon zest
2 bay leaves
½ tsp black peppercorns
480 g / 1 lb ⅞ oz fresh salmon fillet
GRILLED SWEET POTATO
160 g / 5⅝ oz sweet potato
CAESAR DRESSING
2 egg yolks
1½ tsp white wine vinegar
2 tsp mustard
1 tsp anchovies
20 g / ¾ oz / ¼ cup chopped parsley
1 clove garlic, peeled and chopped
100 ml / 3⅜ fl oz / ⅜ cup olive oil
160 g / 5⅝ oz / 1 cup diced mango for garnishing
1 tsp chopped chilli for garnishing
2 tsp chopped mint for garnishing

TEA-SMOKED SALMON Place the tea leaves, sawdust, citrus zest, bay leaves and pepper in a wok and turn up the heat. When it starts to smoke, lower the heat and place the salmon on a metal rack in the wok, above the smoking ingredients. Leave to smoke for 5 minutes. Remove from heat and finish cooking in oven at 60°C / 140°F for 5 minutes. GRILLED SWEET POTATO Cook the sweet potato in boiling salted water. Drain and let cool. Peel and cut into 1-cm / 0.4-inch thick slices. Grill for 30 seconds on each side. CAESAR DRESSING Combine all the dressing ingredients in a bowl and mix well. TO SERVE Cut the salmon into pieces small enough to sit on the pieces of grilled potato. Toss the mango, chilli and mint with the Caesar dressing and garnish the salmon with it.

WINE NV Taittinger Brut, Rheims, France

TEMPURA OF CHINA SEA ANCHOVIES ON DAIKON & SEAWEED PURÉE Serves 8

DAIKON & SEAWEED PURÉE
150 g / 5¼ oz daikon radish, peeled and chopped
8 g / ¼ oz nori, chopped
1 tsp lemon juice
Salt to taste
240 g / 8½ oz cucumber, peeled
TEMPURA BATTER
250 g / 8⅞ oz / 2 cups rice flour
5½ tbsp soda water
1 egg
60 g / 2⅛ oz ice
TEMPURA OF CHINA SEA ANCHOVIES
320 g / 11¼ oz China Sea or other anchovies
Oil for deep-frying

DAIKON & SEAWEED PURÉE Purée the daikon with the nori and a little lemon juice in a blender. Season with salt. Cut the cucumber into 2-cm / 0.8-inch sections and hollow out the centre. TEMPURA BATTER In a bowl, mix all the batter ingredients together. TEMPURA OF CHINA SEA ANCHOVIES Dip the anchovies into the batter and deep-fry in oil until crisp. TO SERVE Place the daikon purée inside the hollow of the cucumber. Top with the fried anchovies.

WINE NV Taittinger Brut, Rheims, France

WILD MUSHROOM FRITTATA WITH ROASTED CHERRY TOMATO SALAD Serves 8

WILD MUSHROOM FRITTATA
60 g / 2⅛ oz onions, peeled and finely diced
3 cloves garlic, peeled and finely diced
Olive oil for frying
80 g / 2⅞ oz button mushrooms, cut into 0.5-cm / 0.2-inch cubes
15 g / ½ oz dried morels, soaked, rinsed and diced into 0.5-cm / 0.2-inch cubes
50 ml / 1¾ fl oz / ¼ cup red wine (cabernet sauvignon)
2 tsp lemon zest
2 tbsp whipping cream
80 g / 2⅞ oz spaghetti
6 eggs, beaten
15 g / ½ oz grated Parmesan
Salt and pepper to taste
ROASTED CHERRY TOMATO SALAD
150 g / 5¼ oz cherry tomatoes, halved
15 g / ½ oz basil, chopped
1 tbsp balsamic vinegar
1 star anise pod
2 tsp chopped basil for garnishing

WILD MUSHROOM FRITTATA In a pot, sauté 10 g / ⅜ oz onions and two-thirds of the garlic in a little olive oil. Add the mushrooms, red wine and lemon zest. Reduce the liquid to a syrupy consistency. Add the cream and reduce further to desired consistency. Let cool. Cook the spaghetti according to instructions. Beat the eggs with the Parmesan and season to taste. Sauté the remaining onions and garlic. Combine with the spaghetti, mushroom mix and eggs and fry until the egg sets. Turn the omelette over and brown the other side. ROASTED CHERRY TOMATO SALAD Place the halved cherry tomatoes on a baking tray with the basil, balsamic vinegar and star anise. Roast at 80°C / 175°F for 40 minutes. TO SERVE Cut the wild mushroom frittata into 2-by-3-by-2-cm / 0.8-by-1.2-by-0.8-inch pieces. Place a piece of tomato on each piece and garnish with chopped basil.

WINE NV Taittinger Brut, Rheims, France

ROASTED CHICKEN ON PUMPKIN & POTATO WITH SOY BEURRE BLANC Serves 2

ROASTED CHICKEN
2 chicken breasts
Salt and pepper to taste
2 tsp lemon zest
PUMPKIN & POTATO
10 g / ⅜ oz shallots, peeled and roasted
Oil for frying
40 g / 1⅜ oz new potatoes
60 g / 2⅛ oz pumpkin, cut into segments
SOY BEURRE BLANC
4 tsp light soy sauce
1 tsp dark soy sauce
12 g / ⅜ oz pickled ginger
1 tbsp whipping cream
60 g / 2⅛ oz butter
SATAY SAUCE
40 g / 1⅜ oz peanuts
12 g / ⅜ oz Thai red curry paste
Oil for frying
1 clove garlic, peeled and finely diced
40 g / 1⅜ oz onions, peeled and finely diced
Thumb-sized piece of fresh ginger, peeled and finely diced
½ tsp oyster sauce
Fish sauce to taste
60 ml / 2 fl oz / ¼ cup coconut milk
12 g / ⅜ oz mint, chopped
12 g / ⅜ oz coriander, chopped
Salt and pepper to taste

ROASTED CHICKEN Season the chicken with salt, pepper and lemon zest. Set aside for 15 minutes. Preheat grill, place the chicken on a hot plate or pan and grill for 10 minutes. Alternatively, bake in a 220°C / 430°F oven for 10 minutes. PUMPKIN & POTATO Preheat oven to 200°C / 400°F. In a pan, fry the shallots in 1 tsp of oil on medium heat for 5 minutes or until they begin to brown. Add the potatoes and mix well. Transfer to a baking dish and bake until potatoes are cooked. Cut the pumpkin into segments. Brush with oil and roast as with potatoes. SOY BEURRE BLANC Mix the light and dark soy sauce with the ginger and reduce by half. Add the cream, reduce again and whisk in butter until well mixed. SATAY SAUCE Dry roast the peanuts on a tray in a 120°C / 250°F oven for 30 minutes. Let them cool a little, and then process them in a blender until powdery. Set aside. Fry the red curry paste with a little oil. Add the garlic, onions, ginger, oyster sauce, fish sauce, coconut milk and powdered peanuts. Mix well before adding the mint and coriander. Season with salt and pepper. TO SERVE Place a portion of vegetables on the pumpkin and the chicken on top of that. Spoon satay sauce over and garnish with coriander.

WINE 2000 Miura Vineyards Carneros Chardonnay, California, USA

CHILLED PRAWNS WITH ROASTED CAPSICUM SALAD Serves 2

BOUILLON
4 tsp white wine (chardonnay)
3 tbsp white vinegar
1 bay leaf
1 tsp chopped onions
2 tsp chopped celery
1 tsp chopped leek
600 ml / 1 pt ¼ fl oz / 2½ cups water
4 white peppercorns
CHILLED PRAWNS
6 jumbo prawns, shelled and deveined
SALAD
20 g / ¾ oz artichoke hearts, soaked in salted water with a few drops of lemon juice
20 g / ¾ oz / ¼ cup corn kernels
60 ml / 2 fl oz / ¼ cup milk
15 g / ½ oz asparagus, blanched and refreshed
15 g / ½ oz watercress, cut into 10-cm / 4-inch pieces
20 g / ¾ oz frisée
A few sprigs of coriander leaves
6 stalks chives
60 ml / 2 fl oz / ¼ cup water
Lemon juice to taste
40 g / 1⅜ oz red capsicum, roasted, peeled, seeded and cut into strips
DRESSING
A pinch of finely diced ginger
Zest from 1 lime
1 tsp mirin
½ tsp vinegar
Salt, pepper and sugar to taste
2½ tsp water
4 tsp olive oil
1 tbsp salmon roe
CHILLI SAUCE
1 tsp lemon juice
60 ml / 2 fl oz / ¼ cup water
½ tsp finely chopped chilli
Sugar to taste
Potato chips for garnishing

BOUILLON Combine all the ingredients in a pot and simmer. CHILLED PRAWNS Poach prawns in the bouillon for 15 minutes at 80°C / 175°F. Remove and chill. SALAD Poach artichokes in the bouillon until tender. Set aside. Boil corn in milk until cooked. Set aside. Put the asparagus, watercress, lettuce, coriander and chives in cold water. Simmer the water, lemon juice and capsicum in a pan until dry. DRESSING Mix the ginger with lime zest. Add the mirin, vinegar, sugar and water and reduce to desired consistency. Strain and add olive oil. When cool, add salmon roe. Season. CHILLI SAUCE Simmer lemon juice, water, chilli and sugar to desired thickness. TO SERVE Toss salad ingredients, except lettuce, with dressing. Arrange the prawns and salad on a bed of lettuce. Serve with chips and chilli sauce.

WINE 2001 Viñedos y Crianzas del Alto Aragón, Enate Unoaked Chardonnay 234, Somontano, Spain

Chilled prawns with roasted capsicum salad.
OPPOSITE: Roasted chicken on pumpkin and potato with soy beurre blanc.

Sun-dried tomato pizza.
OPPOSITE: Mango pizza.

MANGO PIZZA Serves 2

PIZZA DOUGH
60 g / 2⅛ oz butter
120 g / 4¼ oz / 1 cup flour
1 large egg
80 g / 2⅞ oz / ⅝ cup icing sugar
A pinch of salt
CUSTARD SPREAD
400 ml / 13½ fl oz / 1⅔ cups milk
3 egg yolks
2 tbsp sugar
40 g / 1⅜ oz / ¼ cup custard powder
20 g / ¾ oz butter, cut into cubes and chilled
A pinch of lemon zest
TOPPING
400g / 14⅛ oz fresh mango, sliced

PIZZA DOUGH Using your fingertips, rub the butter into the flour to get a sandy texture. Beat the egg, icing sugar and salt. Mix into the dough, kneading lightly. Let the dough rest for 30 minutes in a cool place. CUSTARD SPREAD Heat the milk in a pot to just under boiling point and remove from heat. In another pan, whisk the egg yolks and sugar. When the sugar has dissolved, add the mixture to the hot milk and mix. Return the pot to the stove and bring to a boil. Add the custard powder and whisk in the chilled butter for creaminess. Stir in lemon zest to finish. MANGO PIZZA Preheat oven to 220°C / 430°F. Roll the pastry out into discs with an 8-cm / 3-inch diameter. Spread the custard on top of each disc and top with slices of mango. Bake for 20 minutes or until the pizza base is crisp. TO SERVE Best served hot from the oven.

WINE 1999 Baron Philippe de Rothschild Sauternes, Bordeaux, France

SUN-DRIED TOMATO PIZZA

Serves 2

PIZZA DOUGH
120 g / 4¼ oz / 1 cup flour, sieved
3 tbsp olive oil
240 ml / 8⅛ fl oz / 1 cup iced water
TOMATO CONCASSE
30 g / 1 oz onions, peeled and finely chopped
1 clove garlic, peeled and finely chopped
3 tbsp olive oil
100 g / 3½ oz tomato, peeled, seeds removed and finely chopped
20 g / ¾ oz basil, cut into 1-by-1.5-cm / 0.4-by-0.6-inch strips
60 ml / 2 fl oz / ¼ cup red wine (cabernet sauvignon)
Salt and pepper to taste
A pinch of lemon zest
TOPPING
60 g / 2⅛ oz grated Parmesan
60 g / 2⅛ oz whole sun-dried tomatoes

PIZZA DOUGH Mix the flour, olive oil and iced water into a dough and knead until very elastic. Leave for 30 minutes in a cool place. TOMATO CONCASSE Sauté the onions and garlic in olive oil until the onions are translucent. Add the chopped tomatoes and simmer gently for 3 hours until the mixture turns into a paste. Add the basil and red wine and cook for another 30 minutes to thicken the paste. Season with salt and pepper. Stir in lemon zest. Let cool. SUN-DRIED TOMATO PIZZA Preheat oven to 220°C / 430°F. Roll pizza dough into a disc with a 10-cm / 4-inch diameter. Sprinkle a layer of grated Parmesan over, then spread a layer of tomato concassé on this. Top with sun-dried tomatoes. Finish with another sprinkling of Parmesan and basil. Bake for about 20 minutes or until the pizza base is crisp. TO SERVE Best served hot from the oven.

WINE 2001 Revereto Gavi del Commune di Gavi, Michele Chiarlo, Piedmont, Italy

The roomy verandah at The Pavilion allows diners to make the most of sunny skies and warm breezes during meals; Confit of squid with mango salad. OPPOSITE (FROM LEFT): Coconut poached snapper on curried mixed lentils with bouillabaisse sauce; Vanilla and starfruit parfait.

CONFIT OF SQUID WITH MANGO SALAD Serves 2

CONFIT OF SQUID
4 tbsp oil
160 g / 5⅝ oz whole squid, cleaned
FISH CHILLI SAUCE
4 tsp fish sauce
Juice from 2 limes
4 tsp sugar
4 tsp water
MANGO SALAD
300 g / 10½ oz green mango
10 g / ⅜ oz carrot
10 g / ⅜ oz onions, peeled
40 g / 1⅜ oz basil
40 g / 1⅜ oz ram or celery leaves
1 red chilli
A pinch of thyme leaves
A pinch of lemon zest
A pinch of cinnamon powder
20 g / ¾ oz deep-fried vermicelli for garnishing
2 shrimp crackers for garnishing
1 red chilli, roasted for garnishing

CONFIT OF SQUID Heat the oil to just 60°C / 140°F and cook the squid until it turns white. Set aside on a sheet of kitchen paper to soak up excess oil. FISH CHILLI SAUCE Mix all the ingredients together and set aside. MANGO SALAD Cut the mango, carrot, onions, basil and ram leaves into short, thin strips. In a bowl, mix all the salad ingredients together with the fish chilli sauce and squid. TO SERVE Place the squid and mango salad on a serving plate. Garnish with deep-fried vermicelli, shrimp crackers and roasted chilli.

WINE 2002 McDowell Valley Vineyards Viognier, Mendocino County, California, USA

COCONUT POACHED SNAPPER ON CURRIED MIXED GRAINS WITH BOUILLABAISSE SAUCE

Serves 2

CURRY SAUCE
A pinch of Madras curry powder
A pinch of coriander powder
A pinch of turmeric powder
1 clove garlic, peeled and crushed
12 g / ⅜ oz apple, peeled and thinly sliced
12 g / ⅜ oz leek, sliced
12 g / ⅜ oz onion, peeled and sliced
20 g / ¾ oz tomato, quartered
200 ml / 6¾ fl oz / ⅞ cup coconut water
4 tsp coconut cream
A pinch of garam masala powder
BOUILLABAISSE SAUCE
200 ml / 6¾ fl oz / ⅞ cup snapper fish stock (see Basics)
12 g / ⅜ oz celery, chopped
12 g / ⅜ oz leek, chopped
15 g / ½ oz onions, peeled and chopped
15 g / ½ oz tomato, chopped
40 g / 1⅜ oz navel orange, peeled and chopped
12 g / ⅜ oz dill, chopped
20 g / ¾ oz /¼ cup fennel, chopped
60 g / 2⅛ oz potato, peeled and diced
A pinch of saffron
½ tsp Pernod
WILD GRAINS
20 g / ¾ oz / ⅛ cup uncooked wild rice
60 ml / 2 fl oz / ¼ cup water
60 g / 2⅛ oz / ⅓ cup uncooked white rice
120 ml / 4 fl oz /½ cup water
60 g / 2⅛ oz / ⅓ cup corn kernels
60 g / 2⅛ oz French beans, diced
Salt to taste
COCONUT POACHED GROUPER
350 g / 12⅜ oz snapper fillet, cut into 2 portions
200 ml / 6¾ fl oz / ⅞ cup coconut cream
1 stalk lemon grass, bruised

20 g / ¾ oz tomato, chopped
12 g / ⅜ oz coriander, chopped
ORANGE WAFER
2 very thin orange slices, dried in an oven at 80°C / 175°F for 30 minutes until crisp

CURRY SAUCE In a pot, roast the curry, coriander and turmeric powder with a little oil. Stir for 30 seconds then add the garlic, apple, leek, onion and tomato. Cook for 20 minutes. Add coconut water, mix and heat to just below boiling point. Add coconut milk, simmer until desired consistency, and stir in garam masala powder. BOUILLABAISSE SAUCE Place all the bouillabaisse ingredients except the Pernod in a pot and boil until the potatoes are soft. Mix in the Pernod and transfer everything to a blender. Process until smooth. MIXED GRAINS Put the wild rice and 60 ml / 2 fl oz / ¼ cup of water into a pot, cover and boil until soft. Set aside. Cook the white rice in similar fashion with 120 ml l / 4 fl oz / ½ cup of water. Cook corn and beans until tender in boiling salted water. When cooked, immediately transfer to iced water. COCONUT POACHED SNAPPER Place the snapper in the coconut cream with the lemon grass. Poach until the fish is medium cooked. Remove the fish and set aside. TO SERVE Reheat the curry sauce and add the grains, beans and corn, followed by the chopped tomato and coriander. Place a portion of the curried grains in the centre of each plate. Top with the fish. Pour the bouillabaisse sauce around it and garnish with an orange wafer.

WINE 2001 Domaine E. Guigal Condrieu, Rhône, France

VANILLA & STARFRUIT PARFAIT Serves 2

BISCUIT BASE
120 g / 4¼ oz plain biscuits, broken into crumbs
40 g / 1⅜ oz butter
4 tsp sugar
STARFRUIT PARFAIT
3 egg whites
3 tsp sweet white wine (Sauterne)
A pinch of vanilla beans
60 g / 2⅛ oz / ⅓ cup sugar
5½ tbsp heavy cream
100 g starfruit, peeled and boiled
4 tsp dry white wine (chardonnay)
60 g / 2⅛ oz / ⅓ cup sugar
1 cinnamon stick
A pinch of salt
1 tbsp apricot jam for garnishing
4 thin starfruit slices for garnishing

BISCUIT BASE Mix the biscuits, butter and sugar. Firmly pack half of two 5-cm- / 2-inch-diameter moulds with them. STARFRUIT PARFAIT Whisk the egg whites, sweet white wine, vanilla and sugar in a heat-proof mixing bowl in a bain marie until you can write a clear figure of 8 with the whisk in the mixture. Remove from heat and whisk until cool. In another bowl, whisk the cream until thick. Fold this into the egg mixture. Boil the starfruit in dry white wine, sugar, cinnamon and a little salt until soft. Process in a blender until smooth. Strain through a fine sieve. Combine with egg mixture and fill the moulds. Freeze. TO SERVE Heat the apricot jam and brush the sliced starfruit with it. Unmould parfaît with a warm knife and garnish with starfruit.

WINE 2001 Domaine Louis Sipp Gewürztraminer Vendanges Tardives, Alsace, France

PAN-FRIED DUCK & PAPAYA SALAD WITH CURRIED EEL & GLASS NOODLES Serves 2

FISH SAUCE DRESSING
4 tsp fish sauce
2 limes
4 tsp sugar
4 tsp water
PAPAYA SALAD
200 g / 7 oz papaya, peeled and cut into thin strips
10 g / ⅜ oz white onions, peeled and sliced
60 g / 2⅛ oz basil, cut into thin strips
20 g / ¾ oz ram or celery leaves, cut into thin strips
SPICY SAUCE
½ tsp satay sauce
1 tsp chilli sauce
½ tsp tomato sauce
2 tbsp oyster sauce
PAN-FRIED DUCK
240 g / 8½ oz duck breast
Oil for frying
CURRIED EEL
240 g / 8½ oz eel, skin and bones removed
1 tsp curry powder
GLASS NOODLES
60 g / 2⅛ oz shallots, peeled and finely diced
100 g / 3½ oz onions, peeled and sliced
20 g / ¾ oz / ¼ cup peanuts, crushed
60 g / 2⅛ oz garlic, peeled and finely diced
1 red chilli, sliced
60 g / 2⅛ oz / ⅓ cup sugar
2 stalks lemon grass, white portion finely diced
Oil for frying
40 g / 1⅜ oz ear mushrooms, sliced thinly
200 ml / 6¾ fl oz / ⅞ cup coconut milk
100 g / 3½ oz carrot, peeled and sliced
10 g / ⅜ oz glass noodles, soaked
100 g / 3½ oz snow mushrooms, sliced thinly
100 g / 3½ oz Chinese cabbage, shredded
Salt to taste
2 tsp fried shallot for garnishing
2 red chillies, sliced for garnishing
2 shrimp crackers for garnishing

FISH SAUCE DRESSING Mix all the ingredients. PAPAYA SALAD Marinate the papaya, onions and herbs in the fish sauce dressing. SPICY SAUCE Mix all the ingredients. PAN-FRIED DUCK Sauté the duck in a little oil until medium rare or to desired doneness. Slice and toss in spicy sauce. CURRIED EEL Marinate the eel with curry powder for 3 hours. GLASS NOODLES Fry shallots, onions, peanuts, garlic, chilli, sugar and lemon grass with oil in a clay pot. Add eel, mushrooms and coconut milk and heat to just under boiling point. Add carrots, noodles, mushrooms and cabbage. Cover pot and cook on medium heat for 20 minutes until the eel is tender. Season. TO SERVE Transfer the eel, vegetables, mushrooms and noodles to plates. Top with duck and papaya salad and garnish with fried shallots and chilli. Serve with shrimp crackers and spicy sauce.

WINE 2001 / 2002 Robert Skalli Merlot, Vin de Pays d'Oc, France

The bedrooms combine traditional elements with the best in modern luxury and comfort.
OPPOSITE (FROM REAR): Pan-fried duck and papaya salad with curried eel and glass noodles; Braised ginger chicken; Crispy squid heads.

BRAISED GINGER CHICKEN

Serves 2

BRAISED GINGER CHICKEN
100 g / 3½ oz onions, peeled and sliced thinly
100 g / 3½ oz ginger, peeled and crushed
100 g / 3½ oz spring onions, chopped
3 tbsp sugar
6 chicken drumsticks, deboned and cut into 5-cm / 2-inch pieces
4 tsp tamarind paste
60 g / 2⅛ oz garlic, peeled and sliced thinly
1 tsp fish sauce
100 g / 3½ oz shallots, peeled and sliced thinly
3 tbsp chicken stock (see Basics)
Salt to taste
2 chillies, cut into strips
DIP
4 tsp light soy sauce
1 red chilli, sliced
160 g / 5⅝ oz / 2 cups cooked white rice

BRAISED GINGER CHICKEN Place the onions, ginger and spring onions in a heated clay pot with a little oil. Fry briefly, without letting the onions colour. Add the sugar and continue frying until the onions begin to glaze. Add the chicken and cook until the onions begin to brown. Add the tamarind, garlic, fish sauce, shallots and chicken stock, and mix well. Cover the clay pot and cook on medium heat for about 20 minutes or until the chicken is tender. Season to taste and mix in chilli. DIP Mix the soy sauce with chilli. TO SERVE Serve the chicken with rice and dip on the side.

WINE 2002 Clos du Val Chardonnay, Napa Valley, California, USA

CRISPY SQUID HEADS Serves 2

BATTER
10 g / ⅜ oz onion, peeled and chopped
40 g / 1⅜ oz spring onions, chopped
20 g / ¾ oz ginger, peeled and chopped
2 tsp five spice powder
1 tbsp tamarind powder
2 tsp salt
2 tsp chilli powder
3½ tbsp cornstarch
CRISPY SQUID HEAD
200 g / 7 oz squid heads
Oil for deep-frying
SALAD
20 g / ¾ oz lettuce
20 g / ¾ oz tomato
15 g / ½ oz cucumber
2 sprigs mint
4 stalks coriander
NAM NUOC
1 tsp fish sauce
1 tsp minced chilli
2 tsp sugar

BATTER Mix all ingredients together and leave aside for 1 hour. CRISPY SQUID HEADS Dip the squid heads into the batter and deep-fry in hot oil until they begin to brown. SALAD Slice and combine all the salad ingredients and toss well. NAM NUOC Mix all ingredients together in a sauce dish. TO SERVE Present the crispy squid on the salad and serve with the nam nuoc on the side or drizzled over.

WINE 2002 Springfield Estate Firefinch Ripe Red 'What the Birds Left', Robertson, South Africa

CHEF BUU'S PORK RIB SOUP

Serves 4

CHEF BUU'S PORK RIB SOUP
500 g / 1 lb 1⅝ oz pork ribs, chopped into 15-cm /
6-inch pieces
1 L / 1 pt 14 fl oz / 4¼ cups water
Salt to taste
80 g / 2⅞ oz / ½ cup garlic, peeled and chopped
40 g / 1⅜ oz / ⅓ cup white peppercorns
40 g / 1⅜ oz herb mix for Chinese pork rib soup
3 tbsp dark soy sauce
Salt and sugar to taste
Fresh herbs or vegetables of your choice, cut into
thin strips for garnishing

CHEF BUU'S PORK RIB SOUP Poach the
pork ribs in a pot of simmering salted water for
20 minutes. Transfer the ribs to a pan and fry
with the garlic and white peppercorns without
oil until lightly browned. Return the ribs to the
pot of salted simmering water and poach until
tender. Bring to a boil and add the herb mix.
Lower heat to a simmer and cook for 1½ hours.
Add the dark soy sauce, salt and sugar and
simmer for a further 20 minutes. TO SERVE
Present soup in a bowl, garnished with fresh
herbs or strips of vegetables of your choice.
Best eaten with hot steamed rice.

WINE 2001 Pighin Pinot Grigio, Friuli, Italy

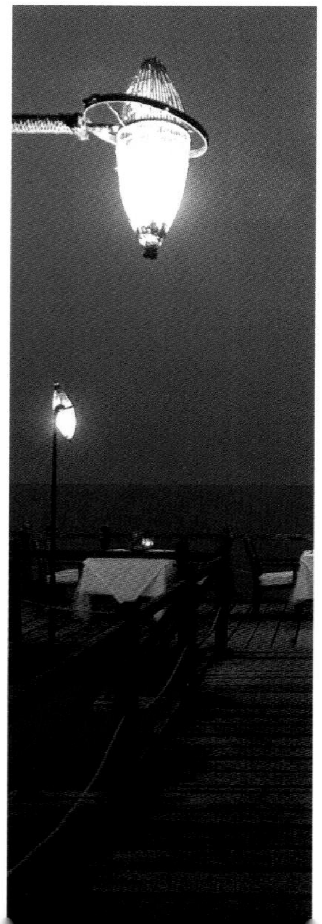

VIETNAMESE PRAWN SPRING ROLLS Serves 4

VIETNAMESE PRAWN SPRING ROLLS
60 g / 2⅛ oz carrots, cut into thin strips
5½ tbsp white vinegar
4 tsp sugar
½ tsp salt
10 sheets rice paper
100 g / 3½ oz lettuce, cut into thin strips
20 g / ¾ oz basil, cut into thin strips
20 g / ¾ oz ram or celery leaves, cut into thin strips
30 g / 1 oz chives, cut into strips
300 g / 10½ oz big prawns, boiled, shells removed
and halved lengthwise
80 g / 2⅞ oz / 1 cup boiled vermicelli
40 g / 1⅜ oz peanuts, roasted and crushed
4 tsp fried shallots
PEANUT SAUCE
100 g / 3½ oz peanuts, roasted and ground to
a powder
50 g / 1¾ oz / ¼ cup sugar
4 tsp salt
2 tbsp coconut milk
100 ml / 3⅜ fl oz / ⅜ cup water
A few lettuce leaves for garnishing
A few stalks spring onions for garnishing
A few slices of lime for garnishing

VIETNAMESE PRAWN SPRING ROLLS
Marinate the carrot strips in vinegar, sugar and
salt for 2 hours. On a sheet of rice paper,
place some carrot, lettuce, herbs, prawns and
vermicelli. Sprinkle with peanuts and fried
shallots. Roll the rice paper around them tightly,
tucking ends in neatly. PEANUT SAUCE Mix
the peanuts, sugar, salt, coconut milk and water
and cook for 30 minutes or until desired
consistency. TO SERVE Present spring rolls on
a bed of lettuce garnished with spring onions
and slices of lime. Serve with peanut sauce on
the side.

WINE 2002 Jackson Estate Sauvignon Blanc,
Marlborough, New Zealand

TAMARIND FISH CURRY Serves 4

TAMARIND FISH CURRY
40 g / 1⅜ oz / ⅛ cup sugar
2 tsp curry powder
Oil for frying
160 g / 5⅝ oz onions, peeled and chopped
40 g / 1⅜ oz garlic, peeled and chopped
1 stalk lemon grass
3 chillies, seeds removed and chopped
400 g / 14⅛ oz eggplant, cut into 2-by-2-by-3-cm /
0.8-by-0.8-by-1-inch pieces
160 g / 5⅝ oz okra, halved
160 g / 5⅝ oz tomatoes, seeds removed and
cut into cubes
300 g / 10½ oz potatoes, peeled and cut
into cubes
320 ml / 10⅞ fl oz / 1⅓ cups coconut milk
3 tbsp fish stock (see Basics)
3 tbsp tamarind paste
600 g / 1 lb 5⅛ oz grouper fillet, 2-by-2-by-3-cm /
0.8-by-0.8-by-1.2-inch pieces
Salt to taste

TAMARIND FISH CURRY Caramelise the
sugar in a heated pot. Add the curry powder
and stir-fry with oil, onions, garlic, lemon grass and
chilli until fragrant. Add the eggplant, okra,
tomatoes and potatoes. Stir-fry for just 2 minutes.
Add the coconut milk, fish stock and tamarind
paste and bring to a boil. Add the fish and cook
until it is done. Adjust seasoning. TO SERVE
Present fish curry and vegetables in a bowl.

WINE 1999 Domaine Antonin Rodet, Château
de Rully, Burgundy, France

The sights and sounds of the sea make
the perfect accompaniment to a quiet
dinner on the jetty.
OPPOSITE (CLOCKWISE FROM TOP): Vietnamese
prawn spring rolls; Tamarind fish curry;
Chef Buu's pork rib soup.

POACHED MARROW & EGGPLANT RISOTTO WITH TOMATO MASALA Serves 2

POACHED MARROW
360 g / 12⅜ oz whole marrow
TOMATO MASALA
60 g / 2⅛ oz tomato, seeds removed and diced
60 g / 2⅛ oz onions, peeled and diced
A pinch of chilli powder
1 bay leaf
1 tbsp oil
EGGPLANT RISOTTO
40 g / 1⅜ oz eggplant, diced
1 clove garlic, peeled and chopped
30 g / 1 oz onions, peeled and chopped
Oil for frying
120 ml / 4 fl oz / ½ cup vegetable stock (see Basics)
2 strips of fresh marrow with skin for garnishing
20 g / ¾ oz Parmesan shavings for garnishing
2 sprigs of basil for garnishing
1 tsp lemon zest for garnishing

POACHED MARROW Place the marrow in aluminium foil and cover with water. Boil until the marrow is tender but firm to the bite. When cool, peel and dice it into 1.5-cm / 0.6-inch cubes. Set aside. TOMATO MASALA Sauté the tomato, onions, bay leaf and chilli powder in oil until the mixture turns into a paste. EGGPLANT RISOTTO Fry the eggplant with garlic and onions in a little oil. Add the vegetable stock and reduce until the eggplant has cooked through. Stir in the tomato masala and mix well. TO SERVE Place a portion of the eggplant risotto and tomato masala on a serving dish. Top with the poached marrow. Garnish with strips of fresh marrow, Parmesan shavings, a sprig of basil and a sprinkling of lemon zest.

WINE 2002 Château La Roque, Bandol, Provence, France

VEGETABLE TEMPURA ON TIAN OF EGGPLANT Serves 2

TIAN OF EGGPLANT
100 g / 3½ oz potatoes, peeled, thinly sliced and blanched
Butter for brushing
200 g / 7 oz eggplant, roasted and sliced
10 g / ⅜ oz basil
100 g / 3½ oz tomato, peeled, seeds removed, diced and drained
1 tsp lemon zest
40 g / 1⅜ oz red capsicum, roasted, peeled and sliced
200 g / 7 oz feta
CAPSICUM SAUCE
50 g / 1¾ oz yellow capsicum, seeds removed and finely diced
2 tbsp water
2 tsp sugar
VEGETABLE TEMPURA
500 g / 1 lb 1⅝ oz / 4 cups tempura flour
150 ml / 5 fl oz / ⅝ cup soda water
40 g / 1⅜ oz ice
2 egg yolks
50 g / 1¾ oz carrot, cut into 8-cm- / 3-inch-long and 0.5-cm / 0.2-inch-wide batons
50 g / 1¾ oz zucchini, cut into 8-cm- / 3-inch-long and 0.5-cm / 0.2-inch-wide batons
50 g / 1¾ oz eggplant, cut into 8-cm- / 3-inch-long and 0.5-cm / 0.2-inch-wide batons
50 g / 1¾ oz onions, peeled and sliced into rings
Oil for deep-frying
2 handfuls of deep-fried rice noodles for garnishing

TIAN OF EGGPLANT Place a layer of sliced potatoes on buttered aluminium foil. Alternate with layers of eggplant, basil, tomato, a sprinkling of lemon zest and red capsicum. When done, crumble the feta along the centre and roll tightly. Rest for 12 hours, occasionally squeezing any liquid out of it during this time. Preheat oven to 300°C / 570°F. Cut the roll into 4-cm / 1.5-inch lengths. Pan-fry on each side, then place on an oven tray and bake for 10 minutes. CAPSICUM SAUCE Boil the yellow capsicum with water and sugar. Blend and strain the sauce through a fine-mesh sieve. Set aside. VEGETABLE TEMPURA Mix the flour, soda water, ice and egg yolks. Dip the carrot, zucchini, eggplant and onions into the batter and deep-fry until crisp. TO SERVE Place the tian of eggplant on a dish and top with a serving of vegetable tempura. Garnish with deep-fried rice noodles and a drizzle of capsicum sauce.

WINE 2003 Springfield Estate 'Life from Stone' Sauvignon Blanc, Robertson, South Africa

Hospitality is a keystone of the Ana Mandara philosophy, and staff are always on hand to welcome guests.
OPPOSITE (FROM LEFT): Poached marrow and eggplant risotto with tomato masala; Vegetable tempura on tian of eggplant.

Privacy can be enjoyed on the secluded beach in front of the hotel, where palm fronds provide ample shade against the sun.
OPPOSITE (FROM LEFT): Marinated scallops with celery and mango sushi; Grilled swordfish with confit of squid and pipperade salad; Fennel salad with olives, tomatoes and spiced cucumber.

MARINATED SCALLOPS WITH CELERY & MANGO SUSHI

Serves 2

CELERY PUREE
160 g / 5⅝ oz celery, cleaned and chopped
60 g / 2⅛ oz onions, peeled and chopped
120 g / 4¼ oz lettuce
2 tsp olive oil
2 tsp virgin olive oil
2 tsp finely grated lemon zest
Salt and pepper to taste
MARINATED SCALLOPS
6 scallops, cleaned
Olive oil for marinating
CELERY & MANGO SUSHI
100 g / 3½ oz / ½ cup Japanese rice, washed
200 ml / 6¾ fl oz / ⅞ cup water
4 tsp vinegar
Salt to taste
2 sheets nori
15 g / ½ oz celery, peeled and sliced into
5-by-1-cm / 2-by-0.4-inch strips
15 g / ½ oz mango, peeled and sliced into
5-by-1-cm / 2-by-0.4-inch strips
Olive oil for garnishing

CELERY PUREE In a blender, purée the celery, onions and lettuce with olive oil, virgin olive oil and lemon zest. Season with salt and pepper, and strain through a fine-mesh sieve. Set aside. MARINATED SCALLOPS Drizzle the scallops with olive oil. Top them with celery purée and grill them or place under a hot salamander until just cooked. Set aside. CELERY & MANGO SUSHI Cook the rice with the water in a rice cooker, then mix it with the vinegar and salt. Place a sheet of nori on a bamboo sushi mat. Spread a layer of rice on the nori. Place a few celery and mango strips on the rice and roll tightly using the bamboo mat. Transfer the roll to a cutting board and slice in half to make 2 servings. Repeat with the other sheet and remaining sushi ingredients. TO SERVE Serve the rolls with the scallops topped with celery purée dressed with a drizzle of olive oil.

WINE NV Mumm Brut, Rheims, France

GRILLED SWORDFISH WITH CONFIT OF SQUID & PIPPERADE SALAD Serves 2

RED CAPSICUM DRESSING
4 tsp balsamic vinegar
60 g / 2⅛ oz red capsicum, peeled and diced
2 tsp sugar
3 tbsp orange juice
GRILLED SWORDFISH
360 g / 12⅜ oz swordfish fillet, halved into 2 squares
Salt and pepper to taste
Olive oil for frying
PIPPERADE SALAD
40 g / 1⅜ oz eggplant, peeled and diced
80 g / 2⅞ oz zucchini, peeled and diced
20 g / ¾ oz green capsicum, peeled and diced
40 g / 1⅜ oz cucumber, peeled and diced
20 g / ¾ oz tomato, peeled and diced
1 clove garlic, peeled and chopped
12 g / ⅜ oz basil, sliced
Salt and pepper to taste
Olive oil for frying
CONFIT OF SQUID
80 g / 2⅞ oz squid, diced
100 ml / 3⅜ fl oz / ⅜ cup olive oil
1 fresh chilli
1 star anise pod
1 cinnamon stick
5 g / ⅛ oz thyme leaves, chopped
2 chillies, seeds removed, cut into strips and soaked in cold water for garnishing
2 lavender flowers for garnishing
2 sprigs thyme for garnishing

RED CAPSICUM DRESSING In a saucepan, reduce the balsamic vinegar over low heat to ½ tsp. Add capsicum, sugar and orange juice and sauté. Reduce to desired consistency. GRILLED SWORDFISH Season the swordfish, then pan-fry with a little oil for 5 minutes on each side. Cut into cubes. PIPPERADE SALAD Sauté all the vegetables with the tomato, garlic and basil. Season. CONFIT OF SQUID Place the squid in oil with the star anise, chilli and cinnamon, and heat to 30°C / 85°F. Cook for 15 minutes at this temperature. TO SERVE Place the squid in a glass dish followed by the salad. Drizzle with dressing and top with the grilled swordfish. Garnish with chilli, lavender and thyme.

WINE 2001 Revereto Gavi del Commune di Gavi, Michele Chiarlo, Piedmont, Italy

FENNEL SALAD WITH OLIVES, TOMATOES & SPICED CUCUMBER Serves 2

FENNEL SALAD WITH OLIVES, TOMATOES & SPICED CUCUMBER
80 g / 2⅞ oz fennel, sliced thinly
80 g / 2⅞ oz asparagus, blanched and cut into
3-cm / 1.2-inch lengths
80 g / 2⅞ oz tomato, seeds removed and diced
40 g / 1⅜ oz cucumber, cut into thick strips
60 g / 2⅛ oz feta, diced
60 g / 2⅛ oz black kalamata olives, pitted and sliced
SALAD DRESSING
4 tsp Dijon mustard
A handful of basil, sliced finely
1 tsp white vinegar
3 tbsp olive oil
Salt and pepper to taste
1 tomato, cut into wedges for garnishing
2 sprigs basil for garnishing

FENNEL SALAD Mix all the salad ingredients together in a large bowl. SALAD DRESSING Combine mustard, basil and vinegar in a bowl and mix well. Slowly stir in the oil. Season with salt and pepper. TO SERVE Toss the salad well with the dressing and serve in 2 glass dishes. Garnish with tomato wedges and basil sprigs.

WINE 2002 Fairview Viognier, Paarl, South Africa

CHICKEN STOCK

Makes about 900 ml / 1 pt 9½ fl oz / 3⅞ cups

1.5 L / 2 pts 11 fl oz / 6⅓ cups water
500 g / 1 lb 1⅝ oz chicken bones
50 g / 1¾ oz ginger
4 to 5 coriander roots
1 white onion, peeled and quartered
1 carrot, cut into large chunks
1 tsp salt

CHICKEN STOCK In a stockpot, bring the water to a boil. Add the chicken bones, ginger and the coriander roots, onion, carrot and salt. Reduce heat and simmer for 30 minutes. Strain and set aside to cool. When cool, chill or freeze until needed.

SEAFOOD STOCK

Makes about 10 L / 16 pts 17 fl oz / 42 cups

100 g / 3½ oz onion, peeled and cut into large chunks
50 g / 1¾ oz celery, cut into large chunks
50 g / 1¾ oz white part of leek, cut into large chunks
3 cloves
2 bay leaves
50 g / 1¾ oz parsley stems
5 g / ⅛ oz fresh thyme
110 g / 3¾ oz mushroom off-cuts
3 tsp salt
3 tbsp lemon juice
100 ml / 3⅜ fl oz / ⅜ cup olive oil
6 kg / 13 lbs 3⅝ oz fish bones, heads, shellfish shells etc., washed
500 ml / 17 fl oz / 2⅛ cups white wine
10 L / 16 pts 17 fl oz / 42 cups water

SEAFOOD STOCK Sauté the vegetables and herbs in a stockpot until glazed. Add the fish bones and shells. Simmer quickly and add the white wine, then add the water. When it is almost boiling, reduce the heat immediately and skim off any foam and fat that surfaces. Let it simmer for no more than 15 minutes, then strain through a fine sieve. Make sure the whole cooking process of the fish bones does not exceed 20 minutes or they will release an unpleasant taste.

VEAL STOCK

Makes about 10 L / 16 pts 17 fl oz / 42 cups

6 kg / 13 lbs 3⅝ oz veal bones
12 L / 20 pts 5 fl oz / 50 cups water
300 g / 10½ oz carrot, cut into large chunks
500 g / 1 lb 1⅝ oz onion, cut into large chunks
225 g / 8 oz celery and leek, cut into large chunks
1 tbsp thyme
5 parsley stems
1 bay leaf
3 cloves
½ tsp white peppercorns, crushed

VEAL STOCK Chop the bones into small pieces and rinse them for about 20 minutes under running water. Place the bones in a pot, cover with cold water and heat until the water boils. Remove them from the water and rinse. Bring them to boil again, this time with the 12 L / 20 pts 5 fl oz / 50 cups of water. Once it starts to boil, reduce the heat to a simmer and skim off any foam that forms. Add the vegetables and herbs. Simmer for about 4 hours while continuing to remove any foam and fat that surfaces. When done, strain repeatedly through a fine muslin.

FISH STOCK

1.5 kg / 3 lbs 4⅞ oz fish bones and well-scaled heads
1 tsp salt
50 g / 1¾ oz onions, peeled and chopped
50 g / 1¾ oz leek, chopped
50 g / 1¾ oz celeriac, peeled and chopped

FISH STOCK Wash the fish parts thoroughly and place them in a stockpot. Add the salt abd vegetables and cover with water. Bring to a boil, then reduce the heat to a simmer. If you want to keep some of the flesh from the heads and bones, take the fish parts out and remove the flesh after this has been cooking for 20 to 25 minutes. Discard bones. Return the flesh to the pot and continue cooking. Simmer stock for 1 hour. Strain stock very carefully through a fine strainer or sieve, ensuring no scales and bones are let through. When cool, chill or freeze until needed.

CHEF'S NOTE After a day, the stock will become a jelly. This is the base for any soup or seafood dishes. If the stock is made a couple of days before use, omit the salt. Unless you freeze it, keep the stock for no more than 2 days.

VEGETABLE STOCK

Makes about 2.5 L / 4 pts 4 fl oz / 10 cups

100 g / 3½ oz onion, peeled and chopped
30 g / 1 oz unsalted butter
80 g / 2⅞ oz white part of leek, chopped
80 g / 2⅞ oz carrots, chopped
60 g / 2⅛ oz celery, chopped
125 g / 4⅜ oz mushrooms, chopped
60 g / 2⅛ oz potato peel
3 L / 5 pts / 12⅔ cups water
50 g / 1¾ oz / ¼ cup lentils
6 cloves garlic, unpeeled
1 tsp black peppercorns
½ tsp thyme leaves
40 g / 1⅜ oz parsley stems
1 bay leaf
1 tsp salt

VEGETABLE STOCK Sauté the onions with butter in a stockpot over medium heat until the onions caramelise. Add the leek, carrots, celery, mushrooms and potato peel and cook until they soften. Add the water, lentils, garlic, peppercorns, thyme, parsley, bay leaf and salt. Bring to a boil, then simmer uncovered for 2 hours. Strain through a fine sieve to get a clear stock. Cool and skim off any foam and fat that surfaces. When cool, chill or freeze until needed.

WASABI MAYONNAISE

Makes about 3 tbsp

1 tsp wasabi powder
1 tbsp water
2 tbsp mayonnaise
Pepper to taste

WASABI MAYONNAISE In a bowl, mix the wasabi powder with water until it is entirely dissolved. Whisk in the mayonnaise until a smooth, slightly thick emulsion is obtained. Season with freshly milled pepper.

PASTA DOUGH

Makes about 1.5 kg / 3 lb 4⅞ oz

550 g / 1lb 3⅜ oz / 4⅓ cups '00' (doppio zero) flour
250 g / 8⅞ oz / 2 cups whole wheat flour
400 g / 14⅛ oz / 3⅛ cups semolina dura
12 eggs
2 tbsp olive oil
Salt to taste

PASTA DOUGH Combine all the ingredients in a small mixing bowl and process with a dough hook until the mixture begins to form a ball. If it is too dry, add a little water. Form dough into a ball and wrap in cling film. Chill in the fridge for at least 2 hours, but not more than 4. After chilling, break off a golf ball-sized piece of dough and pass it through a pasta machine at the thickest setting. Dust with '00' flour to prevent from sticking. Repeat 3 times, reducing thickness setting after each pass. After the 4th time, fold the dough, keeping in mind the width of the machine, and start again at the thickest setting. Repeat until it reaches the thinnest setting. Lay pasta on a pastry board and cut into half. Use half for the ravioli.

DEMI-GLACE

Makes about 250 ml / 8½ fl oz / 1 cup

1.2 kg / 2 lb 10⅜ oz red meat trimmings, coarsely chopped
4 tbsp cooking oil
180 g / 6⅜ oz onions, peeled and diced
60 g / 2⅛ oz leeks, diced
10 cloves garlic
¼ pig's trotter, blanched
2 L / 3 pts 6¾ fl oz / 8½ cups water
2 tbsp butter

DEMI-GLACE Preheat oven to 230°C / 450°F. Brush 1 kg / 2 lb 1¾ oz of the meat trimmings with cooking oil and bake until evenly browned. Add 120 g / 4¼ oz of onions, the leeks and half the garlic and bake for 5 minutes more. Transfer all to a saucepan. Add the pig's trotter, water and the meat juices from the baking pan. Bring to a boil and reduce to a simmer for 2 hours. Remove from heat, strain and transfer to a fresh saucepan. Simmer again to reduce the stock to a quarter of the original volume. Strain again and let cool. Brown the remaining meat trimmings in a pan with butter. Add remaining onions and garlic and fry with 4 tsp of the original lot of demi-glace until their colour changes. Add a third of the remaining demi-glace and reduce the volume by half. Repeat. When adding the last third of the demi-glace, do not reduce. Heat, strain and skim the fat off.

NOTE As a substitute for home-made demi-glace, a rich commercial brown sauce can be used.

CRISPY POTATO WAFERS

Serves 2

1 large potato
Oil for frying

CRISPY POTATO WAFERS Trim the potato into a cylinder about 2.5 cm / 1 inch in diameter. Slice it into thin discs. Set the discs overlapping one another slightly in a lightly oiled non-stick pan with a heavy base. Brush or spray a light layer of oil over the sliced potato. Place a similar sized pan on top of the wafers to keep them flat. Cook it on the stove over medium heat for about 10 to 12 minutes until golden brown and crisp. Remove excess oil by placing them on kitchen paper. When cool, store the wafers in an airtight container to keep them crisp until ready to use.

CUMIN-CRUSTED FILO PASTRY

2 filo pastry sheets
20 g / ¾ oz clarified butter
5 g / ⅛ oz cumin seeds

CUMIN-CRUSTED FILO PASTRY Brush 1 filo sheet with clarified butter. Sprinkle cumin seeds over the entire sheet. Place the second sheet on top and press gently. Cut this into 6 discs of 8 to 10 cm / 3 to 4 inches in diameter. Place the discs on a non-stick tray and bake at 180°C / 350°F for 15 to 20 minutes.

ADOBO SAUCE

A popular Mexican sauce that goes well with a wide variety of meat, seafood and vegetable dishes. It has a distinctively sweet and spicy flavour, and its main ingredients include soy sauce, garlic, vinegar, peanuts, sugar, chillies and other assorted spices.

AMARENA CHERRIES

Sourish bitter wild cherries from Italy, most commonly used for dessert toppings. They are available preserved in syrup or alcohol.

BAIN MARIE

A steam bath used for cooking foods that require gentle heating, like custard and certain sauces. A simple setup comprises a bowl of food placed over a large pan of water, which is then kept at a very low boil.

BASMATI RICE

Long-grain rice from northern India. Its rich fragrance is distinctive whether cooked in briyani dishes or simply steamed on its own.

BAVAROIS

A creamy custard dessert, sometimes described as a mix between a soufflé and a mousse.

BLUE GINGER

Also known as galangal, it is a rhizome related to ginger, with a hot peppery flavour. Most often used as a seasoning, it is particularly popular in Thai cuisine.

BOK CHOY

A Chinese cabbage recognisable by its stout white stalks and long, dark green leaves. It has a slightly peppery flavour, and is used raw in salads, as well as cooked in stir-fried dishes.

BOONDI

A small Indian fritter, made from deep-frying Bengal gram flour batter until it turns crispy. 'Boondi' also refers to the perforated dish that is used to drop the batter into the oil.

BUTTER LETTUCE

Also known as butterhead lettuce. Its small leaves are light green in colour, soft in texture and sweet in taste. It is often preferred by chefs for gourmet preparations. The leaves form loose and delicate heads, and these need to be handled gently when washing.

CEVICHE

Fish or seafood that has been cured with a citric marinade. It is the national dish of Peru, but is also very popular throughout Latin America.

CHAPATTI

An unleavened flat bread from India, made from ground wholemeal flour and water. They can be dipped in curries, or rolled up with a filling.

CHAT MASALA POWDER

A spice mix popular in both northern and southern Indian cuisine, consisting of ground cumin seeds, mango powder, chilli powder, black pepper, garam masala powder and ground black salt. It is characteristically hot and sour in flavour, and its strength gets richer with age.

CHÈVRE

A white cheese which is made from goat's milk, though certain varieties contain cow's milk. It is sharp in flavour, and is available in a variety of shapes and textures.

CHIPOTLE

This is a green or red jalapeño pepper with a characteristically smoky flavour originating from Mexico that has been ripened and dried.

CHORIZO

A type of Spanish salami, strongly flavoured with garlic and paprika, and lightly smoked. They are commonly added to fried and stewed dishes.

CHUTNEY

An Indian condiment made from chopped fruit or vegetables, vinegar, sugar and spices. A few varieties are often laid out at each serving as dips for crackers or flat breads.

COURT-BOUILLON

This is a savoury vegetable stock used in classic French cooking for the preparation of seafood. It typically consists of carrots, celery, herbs and sometimes a little wine.

DHAL

This refers to a range of similar Indian dishes which are made from beans or lentils, tomatoes and assorted spices. Depending on the ingredients, dhals will resemble either a purée or a curry.

DRAGON FRUIT

This is a tropical cactus fruit about the size of two fists held together. It is readily recognisable by its pink skin with soft, floppy scales. Inside, its white flesh is dotted with tiny, edible black seeds.

FRISÉE

A type of lettuce which is popularly used in salads. Its wide but delicate leaves have curly edges that are joined to a short stem. They are most often green in colour, though occasionally seen sporting a red tinge.

GARAM MASALA

This term covers a wide range of spicy powder mixtures in India that vary according to the respective regions. The most common ingredients include black cumin seeds, pepper, turmeric, coriander, cinnamon, cloves and chillies. It is traditionally prepared fresh every morning for the day's cooking needs, though pre-packaged mixes are also available from grocery stores.

GOAT PEPPER

A tiny Indonesian chilli that is very spicy.

GRAM

Also known as the mung bean, it is an edible bean that is high in nutritional value, with a black, yellow or green skin, depending on the variety. It is widely used across Asia to make a wide range of dishes from soups to sweets, and is even added to beverages. Starch from mung beans is used to make vermicelli noodles.

GRAPE SEED OIL

Produced from the grape seeds left after the winemaking process, it contains very low levels of saturated fats, and is used for cooking, dressing salads and making margarine.

GYOZA

Similar to Chinese pot stickers, these are juicy Japanese dumplings that are stuffed with marinated pork and vegetables, which are then pan-fried and steamed.

HON DASHI GRANULES

Japanese konbu and bonito-based soup stock, available in granulated or powder form. Also pre-packaged into teabag-sized sachets.

JAPANESE PICKLED GINGER

Also known as 'gari', these slices of ginger pickled in vinegar are offered in Japanese restaurants to cleanse the palate between different dishes or sushi pieces.

JASMINE TEA

This is most commonly made by scenting green Pouchong tea with jasmine flowers, which makes for a light flavour and refreshing aroma.

JICAMA

A crunchy tuber with brown skin, white flesh and a bulbous shape. It is sometimes referred to as the Mexican potato, and can be eaten both raw as well as lightly roasted.

KALAMATA OLIVES

Also known as calamata olives, these are dark eggplant-coloured olives which originate from Greece. They are cured in wine vinegar and slit so as to absorb the marinade. They are named after the port city of Kalamata, which lies in an olive-growing region in Messinia, Greece.

KATTI

A popular Indian snack, this consists of a flat bread rolled up with a filling of meat or vegetables. A variety of different bread types might be used, from parotha to chappati.

LOLLO ROSSO

A frilly lettuce that is often used in salads for its attractive red colour.

MADRAS CURRY POWDER
A potent curry powder mixture that contains a superlative amount of red chilli powder.

MESCLUN
Sometimes referred to as 'expensive designer greens', this comprises a combination of young leaves and shoots of wild plants including endive, lamb's lettuce, dandelion, rocket, groundsel, chervil, salsify, purslane and oakleaf lettuce. Ready-to-use mixed bags are available from speciality gourmet stores.

MIRIN
A sweet rice wine used in cooking to enhance flavours and give dishes an attractive sheen.

MISO PASTE
A thick bean paste that forms an essential ingredient in Japanese cooking, it is most often used as a soup base or added to stews. It is made from a mixture of soy beans and grains, and is extremely high in nutrition and rich in taste.

MIZUNA
A frilly Oriental green with a firm texture and mild mustard taste.

NAM NUOC
A salty sauce made from fermenting anchovies, which is extremely popular in Thailand. As with soy sauce in Chinese and Japanese cooking, the Thais add nam nuoc to everything, from soups to grilled meat dishes. It is also served as a dip.

NIÇOISE OLIVES
A type of French olive that is dark purple or green in colour, with a milder flavour than the salty Greek varieties.

NORI
These are thin sheets of dried seaweed that are slightly sweet. Commonly used to wrap sushi, they are high in protein and iron, and impart a fragrance when added to hot soups.

OAKLEAF
Available in red and green varieties, these oakleaf-shaped greens have crunchy stems and tender leaves.

PAILLARDE
A piece of meat that has been pounded flat, and then briskly grilled or sautéed.

PANKO
These are coarse crumbs of white bread that have been oven-dried or otherwise dehydrated, and are used in Japanese cooking to coat food before frying.

PAPILLOTE
This refers to food that has been oven-cooked in paper or foil pouches to seal in the moisture and flavour, and shield them from direct heat. The food is served with pouches intact, which diners have to remove. This cooking method is mainly applied to fish, chicken and vegetables.

POLENTA
This is a dish of cornmeal cooked in water or stock, and sometimes flavoured with butter or cheese and fried afterwards. It still remains a popular substitute for pasta in northern Italy.

PONZU VINEGAR
A Japanese dipping sauce that contains sweet rice wine, seaweed, rice vinegar and soy sauce.

PORCINI (DRIED)
Porcini are meaty yellow mushrooms favoured in Italian cooking for their flavour and versatility, and are most frequently used in stews, sauces and salads. Dried porcini need to be soaked and rinsed before cooking. Their flavour will be retained in the water, which can also be strained and used as a stock.

PURPLE BASIL
These leaves impart a subtler flavour compared to green basil, and are used to add colour to dishes.

RAU RAM LEAVES
Also known as Vietnamese coriander, they have a pleasant minty flavour and is used to dress Vietnamese dishes.

RED CORAL
A lettuce variety that resembles a red coral. Its leaves are distinctively sweet in flavour.

ROUILLE
A hearty sauce made of garlic, dried chilli, olive oil and sometimes tomato.

SABAYON
Also known as zabaglione in Italian, it is a dessert sauce made by whisking egg yolks, caster sugar and wine or liqueur together until the mixture is thick and fluffy. It can be served hot or cold.

SAKE
A fermented rice alcohol that is also used extensively in Japanese cooking to marinate food and add flavour to sauces.

SAMBAL OELEK
A spicy chilli paste containing salt, vinegar, garlic and sometimes tamarind.

SATAY
A favourite in Singapore and Malaysia, this refers to pieces of beef, chicken or pork skewered on bamboo sticks and cooked over a charcoal grill. These are then dipped in a peanut-based sauce, and eaten with steamed rice cakes, cucumber and raw onions. Originally found at roadside stalls, it can now also be easily found at restaurants.

SOM TAM
A Thai salad made with unripe papaya which has been peeled, shredded and pounded. It is then tossed with chilli, dried shrimp, garlic, fish sauce and a variable assortment of local ingredients.

SZECHUAN PEPPER
This refers to the dried berries of the prickly ash tree, which feature prominently in Chinese five spice powder. These mild peppercorns are traditionally lightly toasted, crushed to release their flavour, then added to dishes.

TAHINI PASTE/SAUCE
A Middle Eastern paste made from sesame seeds and used as a flavouring. The sauce is used as a condiment or dressing.

TAMARI SOY SAUCE
A Japanese soy sauce that has been brewed without wheat or rice, and is thicker and stronger in flavour than the normal variety.

TAPENADE
A purée or spread made from anchovies, garlic, capers and black or green olives. This can be either spread on crackers, served on the side with seafood or meat, or added into sauces and stews.

TIAN
This refers both to a casserole of stewed vegetables that originated in Provence, France, as well as the type of baking dish used to cook it.

TUILE
A thin cookie made with crushed almonds resembling a curved roof tile, moulded by placing over a rounded object such as a rolling pin while still hot from the oven.

WANTON
Bite-sized Chinese dumplings stuffed with minced pork and typically boiled in soup, though they can also be deep-fried.

WASABI
This is prepared from the roots of the Japanese horseradish, which are ground into a green paste. Fresh wasabi is a highly sought-after and very expensive ingredient served mainly in the top restaurants and sushi bars of Japan. As a characteristically Japanese spice, this spicy condiment can be served alongside sushi, sashimi and noodle dishes.

WITLOF
Known as chicory or Belgian endives, witlof is a type of lettuce with cigar-shaped, cream-coloured leaves which taste slightly bitter. These are sometimes brewed to make a beverage.

Appetisers
- baked snapper with green tea noodles and lime salsa 84
- carpaccio of ahi tuna with red capsicum salsa and caramelised mango 64
- char-grilled organic vegetables 32
- deep-fried sesame-crusted prawns, guacamole and organic salad with beetroot vinaigrette 47
- gazpacho with steamed crayfish medallions 53
- green tea noodle sushi with cucumber, avocado and wasabi mayonnaise 83
- marinated scallops with celery and mango 132
- mas roshi (smoked tuna in pastry shell) 28
- pot stickers 112
- salmon trout confit and spicy eggplant with calamansi lime and butter sauce 87
- seared lemon grass and lime leaf-crusted wahoo with rosehip sorbet and apricot compôte 66
- sweet potato risotto with seared scallops and mushrooms 104
- tandoor goat cheese and baked eggplant purée with mint coulis 31
- Thai vegetable crudité with dip 108

avocado pico de gallo purée canapés 99

B
Baked buckwheat crêpes with pumpkin-basil ragôut 31
baked new potato and smoked salmon with dill cream 39
baked snapper with green tea noodles and lime salsa 84
basil-crusted veal tenderloin and yellow lentil ragôut with cinnamon jus 23
blackened prawns with spicy mango 59
beef fillet and shiitake mushrooms in miso sauce with white bean and coriander mash 80
braised ginger chicken 127
Brie, walnut and fruit canapés 99
broiled salmon in miso sauce with crispy bitter vegetables, Japanese mushrooms and soba 63

C
Cappuccino of celery, leek and Spanish onion with pesto 44
caramelised lemon tart 104
carpaccio of ahi tuna with red capsicum salsa and caramelised mango 64
char-grilled chicken and artichoke basmati rice with balsamic vinegar jus 43
char-grilled organic vegetables 32
Chef Buu's pork rib soup 128
chermoulah-spiced tiger prawns with avocado coriander mash 64

chicken
- braised ginger chicken 127
- char-grilled chicken and artichoke basmati rice with balsamic vinegar jus 43
- chicken katti roll 39
- coconut cappuccino and roast chicken with truffles 27
- kai himmapan (stir-fried chicken and cashews) 88
- roasted chicken on pumpkin and potato with soy beurre blanc 120
- spiced risotto with roast chicken, chorizo and ratatouille baked in claypots 68

chicken katti roll 39
chilled prawns with roasted capsicum salad 120
chocolate and mascarpone fritters with orange and ginger compôte 23
citrus and jicama som tam with grilled prawns 107
coconut and vanilla crème brulée in coconut shell 43
coconut cappuccino and roast chicken with truffles 27
coconut poached snapper on curried lentils with bouillabaisse sauce 125

coconut soup with prawns 108
coconut truffle froth with roasted artichokes, buckwheat noodles and zucchini mash 71
confit of squid with mango salad 124

crab
- crabmeat and prawn roe canapés 99
- pan-fried mini Maldivian crab cakes 39
- Thai crab cakes with chilli sauce 79
- crabmeat and prawn roe canapés 99

crispy skinned salmon, mashed potato and mesclun salad with saffron-pepper jus 107
crispy squid head with tamarind sauce 127
cumin-coated beef tenderloin with Madras curry sauce 27
curried lobster tail, soft potato rouille with cumin-crusted filo pastry and artichoke salad 60

curry
- katela riha (sweet potato curry) 28
- red duck curry 108
- roasted black cod and gazpacho hash with red curry sabayon 87
- tamarind fish curry 128

D
Deep-fried red lentil-crusted prawns 19
deep-fried sesame-crusted prawns, guacamole and organic salad with beetroot vinaigrette 47

desserts
- caramelised lemon tart 104
- chocolate and mascarpone fritters with orange and ginger compôte 23
- coconut and vanilla crème brulée in coconut shell 43
- crispy squid head with tamarind sauce 127
- donkeyo kajoo (banana fritters) 28
- flourless chocolate cake with liquorice ice cream 32
- fresh sliced tropical fruit with citrus sorbet 112
- fruit sushi with raspberry and green tea coulis 44
- grilled pineapple with mango, ginger and chilli sorbet 84
- hot chocolate and Bailey's fondue 49
- hot chocolate soufflé with mango and mint ice cream 51
- hot melting chocolate pudding with mirin and ginger sabayon 24
- iced soufflé of yoghurt and berries with toffee sauce 27
- jasmine-flavoured bitter chocolate teacup with prune sorbet 31
- jasmine tea-flavoured chocolate pots with spiced pineapple 63
- kaffir lime-basil parfait with pineapple compôte 87
- kruay chu'am (caramelised bananas) 88
- lime and green tea tiramisu 83
- mango and sticky rice 108
- mango pizza 123
- panko and macadamia-crusted banana spring rolls 111
- pumpkin custard 107
- red wild forest fruit soup with sweet black olives and yoghurt sorbet 53
- saffron-white and five spice dark chocolate mousse cone 64
- spiced pineapple with kulfi ice cream 47
- Thai basil ice cream with fruit compôte 103
- tian of macerated raspberries and raspberry bavarois 67
- vanilla and starfruit parfait 125

Dijon marinated lamb with Thai ratatouille 104
donkeyo kajoo (banana fritters) 28

duck
- red duck curry 108
- roasted duck breast rolled in goat cheese and pine nuts, with crispy duck and rocket salad 39
- pan-fried duck and papaya salad with curried eel and glass noodles 127

F
Fathu satani (lettuce, tomato and onion salad) 28
fehunumas (Maldivian-style baked fish) 28
fennel salad with olives, tomatoes and spiced cucumber 132

fish
- baked snapper with green tea noodles and lime salsa 84
- carpaccio of ahi tuna with red capsicum salsa and caramelised mango 64
- coconut poached snapper on curried lentils with bouillabaisse sauce 125
- fehunumas (Maldivian-style baked fish) 28
- garudhiya (Maldivian tuna soup) 28
- grilled swordfish with confit of squid and pipperade salad 132
- grilled yellow fin tuna steak and sautéed mixed vegetables with mango and pomegranate salsa 40
- herb-crusted Maldivian white tuna, orange-infused chèvre and curried papaya chutney 25
- mas roshi (smoked tuna in pastry shell) 28
- nage of white miso with mussels, scallops, red snapper and river prawns 80
- orange-infused rainbow runner and celeriac potato mash with sweet capsicums 20
- papillote of reef fish and vegetable tagliatelle with lemon oil and fresh herb pesto 53
- poached ginger and lemon grass jackfish with soft polenta and honey-carrot sauce 32
- roasted black cod and gazpacho hash with red curry sabayon 87
- salmon trout confit and spicy eggplant with calamansi lime and butter sauce 87
- seared lemon grass and lime leaf-crusted wahoo with rosehip sorbet and apricot compôte 66
- seared ocean tuna steak and curried potato with garlic, ginger and soy sauce 20
- steamed roll of reef fish and mushrooms with coriander milk sauce 40
- tamarind fish curry 128
- tempura of China Sea anchovies on daïkon and seaweed purée 119
- tod man pla (Thai fish cakes) 88
- wahoo ceviche and fresh coriander on toast 39

flourless chocolate cake with liquorice ice cream 32
fresh sliced tropical fruit with citrus sorbet 112
fruit salad 108
fruit sushi with raspberry and green tea coulis 44

G
Gabulhe (dhal salad) 28
garudhiya (Maldivian tuna soup) 28
gazpacho with steamed crayfish medallions 53
green asparagus velouté with white truffle oil and tomato tartare 51
green tea noodle sushi with cucumber, avocado and wasabi mayonnaise 83
grilled pineapple with mango, ginger and chilli sorbet 84
grilled swordfish with confit of squid and pipperade salad 132
grilled vegetable paella with basil tomato slaw 112
grilled yellow fin tuna steak and sautéed mixed vegetables with mango and pomegranate salsa 40

H
Herb-crusted Maldivian white tuna, orange-infused chèvre and curried papaya chutney 25
hot chocolate and Bailey's fondue 49
hot chocolate soufflé with mango and mint ice cream 51
hot melting chocolate pudding with mirin and ginger sabayon 24

I
Iced soufflé of yoghurt and berries with toffee sauce 27

J
Jasmine-flavoured bitter chocolate teacup with prune sorbet 31
jasmine tea-flavoured chocolate pots with spiced pineapple 63

K
Kaffir lime-basil parfait with pineapple compôte 87
kai himmapan (stir-fried chicken and cashews) 88
katela riha (sweet potato curry) 28
kruay chu'am (caramelised bananas) 88

L
Lamb
- Dijon marinated lamb with Thai ratatouille 104
- roasted rack of lamb and eggplant caviar with tamarind-port sauce 84
- tian of lamb loin with grilled Mediterranean vegetables and goat cheese 59

lemon grass lasagna with organic vegetables and coconut béchamel sauce 91
lime and green tea tiramisu 83

lobster
- curried lobster tail, soft potato rouille with cumin-crusted filo pastry and artichoke salad 60
- lobster tail cocktail with apple-lime leaf compôte and red capsicum sorbet 59
- stir-fried lobster with garlic and pepper 108
- wok-seared lobster with mango 112

lobster tail cocktail with apple-lime leaf compôte and red capsicum sorbet 59

M
Main courses
- baked buckwheat crêpes with pumpkin-basil ragôut 31
- basil-crusted veal tenderloin and yellow lentil ragôut with cinnamon jus 23
- beef fillet and shiitake mushrooms in miso sauce with white bean and coriander mash 80
- broiled salmon in miso sauce with crispy bitter vegetables, Japanese mushrooms and soba 63
- char-grilled chicken and artichoke basmati rice with balsamic vinegar jus 43
- chermoulah-spiced tiger prawns with avocado coriander mash 64
- chilled prawns with roasted capsicum salad 120
- coconut poached snapper on curried lentils with bouillabaisse sauce 125
- coconut truffle froth with roasted artichokes, buckwheat noodles and zucchini mash 71
- crispy skinned salmon, mashed potato and mesclun salad with saffron-pepper jus 107
- cumin-coated beef tenderloin with Madras curry sauce 27
- curried lobster tail, soft potato rouille with cumin-crusted filo pastry and artichoke salad 60
- Dijon marinated lamb with Thai ratatouille 104
- fehunumas (Maldivian-style baked fish) 28
- grilled swordfish with confit of squid and pipperade salad 132
- grilled yellow fin tuna steak and sautéed mixed vegetables with mango and pomegranate salsa 40
- grilled vegetable paella with basil tomato slaw 112
- herb-crusted Maldivian white tuna, orange-infused chèvre and curried papaya chutney 25
- lemon grass lasagna with organic vegetables and coconut béchamel sauce 91
- orange-infused rainbow runner and celeriac potato mash with sweet capsicums 20
- panko-crusted salmon roll and grilled shiitake

SONEVA FUSHI RESORT
& SIX SENSES SPA

SONEVA FUSHI RESORT & SIX SENSES SPA

Tel: +960.230 304

Fax: +960.230 374

Email: reservations-fushi@sonevaresorts.com

SONEVA GILI RESORT
& SIX SENSES SPA

SONEVA GILI RESORT & SIX SENSES SPA

Tel: +960.440 304

Fax: +960.440 305

Email: reservations-gili@sonevaresorts.com

SILA EVASON HIDEAWAY
& SPA AT SAMUI

SILA EVASON HIDEAWAY & SPA AT SAMUI

Tel: +66.77.245 678

Fax: +66.77.245 671

Email: reservations-samui@evasonhideaways.com

EVASON PHUKET RESORT
& SIX SENSES SPA

EVASON PHUKET RESORT & SIX SENSES SPA

Tel: +66.76.381 010

Fax: +66.76.381 018

Email: reservations-phuket@evasonresorts.com

EVASON HUA HIN RESORT
& SIX SENSES SPA

EVASON HUA HIN RESORT & SIX SENSES SPA

Tel: +66.32.632 111

Fax: +66.32.632 112

Email: reservations-huahin@evasonresorts.com

EVASON HIDEAWAY
& SIX SENSES SPA AT HUA HIN

EVASON HIDEAWAY & SIX SENSES SPA AT HUA HIN

Tel: +66.32.618 200

Fax: +66.32.618 201

Email: reservations-huahin@evasonhideaways.com

ANA MANDARA RESORT
AN EVASON RESORT & SIX SENSES SPA

ANA MANDARA RESORT & SIX SENSES SPA

Tel: +84.58.829 829

Fax: +84.58.829 629

Email: reservations-anamandara@evasonresorts.com

EVASON HIDEAWAY
& SIX SENSES SPA AT ANA MANDARA

EVASON HIDEAWAY & SIX SENSES SPA AT ANA MANDARA

Tel: +84.58.829 829

Fax: +84.58.829 629

Email: reservations-anamandara@evasonhideaways.com

ADDITIONAL PHOTO CREDITS

DAN KULLBERG / front flap, 13, 92 • KIATTIPONG PANCHEE / 4, 5, 12, 54–57, 59, 63, 64, 66 (left), 68, 71, 72, 74–75, 77, 84, 99, 117, 119, 124 (left), 131

HENELE PÉ/SKÖNA HEM / 97, 107 • CHAIYOS PHONSUWAN / 39, 43, 104 • ULLI SCHONART / 10, 16 (right), 23, 36, 37, 44, 108

AKIRA TATEISHI / 8–9 • JEAN MARC TINGUAD / 31 • MEMO ZACK / 76